The Relevance
Of Revelation

Thirty-One Days to Radical Revival

JUDY SALISBURY

LOGOS PRESENTATIONS
EQUIPPING – MOTIVATING – LIFE CHANGING

The Relevance of Revelation
Thirty-One Days to Radical Revival
by Judy Salisbury

Copyright © 2021 by Judith A. Salisbury.

Published by Logos Presentations
Woodland, WA 98674

Printed in the United States of America.

ISBN: 9798743401635

DEDICATED TO:

COTR's Cultivate 2.0-E Group

Thank you for making my group leadership
task so enjoyable. I pray you found our time
together profitable for our Lord's service.
You are all such a blessing to me.
Thank you for your prayers for this work!
That is the only way to get it done.
Stay motivated and equipped
as you mature in Him.
God bless you all!

CONTENTS

INTRODUCTION

It seems fitting for me to explain how I came to the idea for a devotional-sized resource utilizing the book of Revelation as a foundation. In February 2021, I was asked to lead a study group on the basics of helping ground participants in the Word of God. The study materials suggested the participants select a book in the Bible to read during their quiet time with the Lord. The materials indicated that, for beginners, they bypass the books of Leviticus and Revelation as a starting point. To this, I was aghast, and my group, who were relatively mature believers, agreed.

To bypass Leviticus would be to miss an explanation as to why a blood sacrifice for atonement is necessary, among many other essential lessons the Holy Spirit would not want us to ignore.

For my participants to dismiss the possibility of delving into the book of *The Revelation of Jesus Christ*, I considered it a missed opportunity to learn much more than the obvious eschatological matters that one considers when approaching Revelation. Instead, I suggested they seek the Holy Spirit's guidance, and if they felt led to start with Revelation or Leviticus, well, more power to them—literally!

During our weekly meetings, we would share what the Lord taught us during our quiet time in the book of the Bible that we had each chosen. Me, being the passive-aggressive that I am (just kidding), I selected the book of Revelation. I desired to show the group that there is much more in this work than trumpet and bowl judgments, or arguments over pre, post, pan, or amillennialism, or how and when the rapture would occur.

During my drive home one night after one of our sessions, I began chatting with the Lord about the suggestion to set aside two essential books of the Bible, even for the novice believer.

"Lord," I said, "I want them to realize just how relevant the book of Revelation is and how it relates to everyday life here and now. It is so rich and full! Help me to show them what else You have to say for us today."

Just then, as I was listening to my praise music, George Frideric Handel's *The Hallelujah Chorus* began to play, and I fell apart. Realizing that if Handel had taken the advice of the individuals who wrote those materials, he might not have created the most inspired piece of music ever written, along with *Worthy is the*

Lamb, as these works were based entirely on passages from the book of Revelation.

Tears streamed down my face as I realized that the Lord was indeed calling me to write, not a treatise of the end times, but a practical resource for today on a book containing events that will *shortly take place* as they unfold in a short amount of time.

My hope is that this little book would not only encourage and enlighten you in these the last days but also that you would be prepared and feel free to delve into all of God's Word no matter how intimidating you might think or even against the recommendations of learned theologians and teachers who author Bible study materials.

Thank you for taking the time to read this work. I pray you will find these thirty-one days of study a blessing as you realize how relevant and practical God's Word is for our lives today and into eternity. May the *KING OF KINGS AND LORD OF LORDS* richly bless you!

Judy Salisbury, May 2021

BEHOLD, HE IS COMING WITH THE CLOUDS,
and every eye will see Him, even those who
pierced Him; and all the tribes of the earth will
mourn over Him. So it is to be. Amen.
Revelation 1:7

———— ⌀⌀ ————

DAY 1 ~ I, JOHN, THE EYEWITNESS

John was an eyewitness. During our Lord's three-year ministry, John the Apostle witnessed His array of miracles and His transfiguration as Jesus talked with Moses and Elijah.[1] John heard the voice of the Father confirm, *"This is My Son, My Chosen One; listen to Him!"*[2] John witnessed the eventual betrayal of Jesus, His arrest, torture from head to toe on a cruel cross, and His incredible words as He hung there, *"Father, forgive them; for they do not know what they are doing."*[3] John was there to testify of Jesus' glorious resurrection, forty days of His inspired teaching,[4] and then His ascension into heaven.

Based upon the Apostle's eyewitness testimony, he wrote with authority the Gospel of John and his three epistles. In 1 John, we find these remarkable words, which drove this author to her knees in repentance in 1991. You

---

[1] Like 9:28-32
[2] Luke 9:35
[3] Luke 23:34
[4] Acts 1:3

see, I realized I could not argue with an eyewitness.

What was from the beginning, what we have heard, what we have seen with our eyes, what we have looked at and touched with our hands, concerning the Word of Life—and the life was manifested, and we have seen and testify and proclaim to you the eternal life, which was with the Father and was manifested to us—what we have seen and heard we proclaim to you also, so that you too may have fellowship with us; and indeed our fellowship is with the Father, and with His Son Jesus Christ.[5]

Perhaps John would never have imagined what the Lord would reveal to him on the Island of Patmos. And yet, why was he there? Vacation? No. It was *because of the word of God and the testimony of Jesus.*[6] In addition to inmate status on Patmos, John suffered not death at the hands of persecutors as the rest of the apostles had, but the torture of being boiled in hot oil. John, who our Lord charged with the responsibility of His mother's care, would eventually be released from Patmos, minister in Ephesus, and die a very old man. However, his release from Patmos would not happen until he

---

[5] 1 John 1:1-3
[6] Revelation 1:9

had witnessed what would be an incredible experience of his very long life—*The Revelation of Jesus Christ*.

The truth is, when we consider it, only an eyewitness could endure the oil, persecution, exile, imprisonment, and eventual death with a consistent message because it came from one who lived it.

The fact is we who live this life in Him are eyewitnesses as well. We have first-hand knowledge of our life before Christ and after. We had witnessed His answers to prayer when we knew the answer could have come no other way but by His hand. It is because of these facts, these *many convincing proofs*[7] in our own lives, that we have a duty and responsibility to fulfill Jesus' call to *"Go into all the world and preach the gospel to all creation."*[8]

Will we face persecution? Are we ready? Is He worth it? Ponder these things today and realize the responsibility of an eyewitness. Then consider it yours.

"In the world you have tribulation, but take courage; I have overcome the world."
John 16:33

---

[7] Acts 1:3
[8] Mark 16:15

When I saw Him,
I fell at His feet like a dead man.
Revelation 1:17

———— ⌒✦⌒ ————

DAY 2 ~ A REVERENT RESPONSE

Speaking of our Lord Jesus Christ, the Apostle John began his Gospel informing, *In the beginning was the Word, and the Word was with God, and the Word was God.*[9]

Jesus, Himself, revealed, *"I assure you, most solemnly I tell you, before Abraham was born, I AM."*[10] At this stunning statement, the response of those who hated Him was to stone Him right there on the spot. Why was that? Because they realized what Jesus was saying of Himself. That He was and is the *I AM* of the burning bush spoken of in Exodus[11] and that indeed, in Jesus *all the fullness of Deity dwells in bodily form.*[12]

We are reminded that while He walked among us that *although He existed in the form of God, did not regard equality with God a thing to be grasped, but emptied Himself, taking the form of a bond-servant, and being made in*

---

[9] John 1:1
[10] John 8:58 (AMP)
[11] Exodus 3:14
[12] Colossians 2:9

5

the likeness of men.[13]

As we search the Scriptures, we find that the individuals who had a glimpse of Christ's majesty or came to the realization that He was Who He said He was, were the ones who responded most reverently.

After a somewhat skeptical professional angler witnessed how Jesus could gather as many fish as He wanted, whenever He wanted, Peter *fell down at Jesus' feet, saying, "Go away from me Lord, for I am a sinful man!"*[14]

When Jesus informed Nathaniel that He "saw" him under a fig tree before they had met, he responded, *"Rabbi, You are the Son of God; You are the King of Israel."*[15]

The centurion from Capernaum, whose servant was ill, stated confidently, *"Lord, I am not worthy for You to come under my roof, but just say the word, and my servant will be healed."*[16] Jesus then commended him for the appropriateness of His great humility and faith, stating, *"Truly I say to you, I have not found such great faith with anyone in Israel."*[17]

Upon seeing the risen Lord, *Thomas answered and said to Him, "My Lord and my God!"*[18] Did Jesus rebuke Thomas for blaspheme? He did not. *Jesus said to him,*

---

[13] Philippians 2:6-7
[14] Luke 5:8
[15] John 1:49
[16] Matthew 8:8
[17] Matthew 8:10
[18] John 20:28

"Because you have seen Me, have you believed? Blessed are they who did not see, and yet believed."[19] Then, there is John on Patmos, with a description of our Lord unparalleled.

I saw one like a son of man, clothed in a robe reaching to the feet, and girded across His chest with a golden sash. His head and His hair were white like white wool, like snow; and His eyes were like a flame of fire. His feet were like burnished bronze, when it has been made to glow in a furnace, and His voice was like the sound of many waters. In His right hand He held seven stars, and out of His mouth came a sharp two-edged sword; and His face was like the sun shining in its strength.[20]

The Apostle John's response was our opening verse for today. Entirely appropriate.

In the 1960s, A.W. Tozer made a stunning admission. *"It is my opinion that the Christian conception of God current in these middle years of the twentieth century is so decadent as to be utterly beneath the dignity of the Most High God and actually to constitute for professed believers something amounting to a moral calamity."*[21]

And what of this, the twenty-first century? It

---

[19] John 20:29
[20] Revelation 1:13-16
[21] https://www.cmalliance.org/devotions/tozer?id=1300

certainly holds that *"Those that never had a sense of their own vileness, were always destitute of a sense of God's holiness."*[22] Perhaps that's the challenge. The farther away we move from a biblical image of God, and the more comfortable we become with our sinful nature, the more casual we grow in our view and approach to God. Somehow, we forget that though we have received forgiveness in Him and He loves us so thoroughly, the realization of Christ's holiness, power, majesty, and as we read in the book of Revelation, justice deserves our awe, humility, and heartfelt reverence in His presence.

Has your reverence waned? What will be your response when you see Jesus face to face? Like John, do you imagine falling on your face before Him? Or do you think your response will be a casual one? If you feel your awe and reverence for our Lord has diminished, take time to consider what I shared today. Whether standing before Him now or in eternity, remember that Jesus is God. Express the honor He is so due, today and always, and be blessed.

Then I (John) fell at his feet to worship him.
But he said to me, "Do not do that; I am a fellow
servant of yours and your brethren who hold the
testimony of Jesus; worship God."
Revelation 19:10

---

[22] Stephen Charnock (1628–1680), *The Existence and Attributes of God,* vol. 2, reprint ed. (Grand Rapids, MI: Baker Books, 1996), p. 192

"I know your deeds..."
Revelation 2:2, 19, 3:1, 8, 15

———⌒✦⌒———

DAY 3 ~ A LITTLE LEAVEN

As we find in Revelation 1:20, Jesus walked among *the seven golden lampstands*, which symbolizes the churches. Christ was well aware of their perseverance and compromise, works great and small, and whether they had a zeal for God or were putridly lukewarm. How comforting it is to know that the service the Lord calls us to, so often unseen and unrecognized by anyone else, does not go beyond His notice.

There is a beautiful intimacy in this image of Jesus walking among these fellowships as gardeners would throughout their beloved orchard. As they stroll about, they can appreciate the beauty, pruning as they go and plucking weeds that could choke out what they lovingly and painstakingly planted there.

The knowledge that such a great God sees our works that are a blessing to Him when done according to His will is enough to satisfy our hearts. Praise from another human being, or a theater full of them standing in ovation, pales in comparison.

In these the last days, as we toil in the Lord,

we can so easily forget that pleasing Him alone is enough. Often, we can feel overwhelmed by the evil we see about us and feel our attempted impact cannot be of any significance. Then we read those powerful and astonishing words in our opening verse today. *"I know your deeds."*

If our great God has called us to it, then what we do on His behalf will not be as though we were spinning our wheels in futility. Again, it will certainly not go beyond His notice. Such was the case with the church in Ephesus. Jesus, walking among them, offered the following commendation:

> I know your industry and activities, laborious toil and trouble, and your patient endurance, and how you cannot tolerate wicked [men] and have tested and critically appraised those who call [themselves] apostles (special messengers of Christ) and yet are not, and have found them to be impostors and liars.[23]

To test and critically appraise a potential imposter and liar takes diligent toil in His Word. Oh, that the Church today would follow the footsteps of the Ephesian fellowship regarding those who call attention to themselves and away from Christ, whether wittingly or unwittingly. Their motives might be

---

[23] Revelation 2:2 (AMP)

sincere, or perhaps *they have a zeal for God, but not in accordance with knowledge.*[24] Whatever the case, when we hear a perversion of God's Word, just as those in the Ephesian fellowship, we cannot ignore it.

The more grounded and mature you become in God's Word, the more you will have the ability to spot any manipulation of it. If this happens in your fellowship, please do not sit silently by and excuse it. Do not question motives; instead, lovingly expose the error. This practice is not easy, and it surely is not popular today. However, it is something our Lord sees, commends, and rewards. We must be on alert, brave, and expose any twisting of Scripture, realizing that, as Paul warned us, *a little leaven leavens the whole lump of dough.*[25]

Yet you have this [in your favor and to your credit]: you hate the works of the Nicolaitans [what they are doing as corrupters of the people], which I Myself also detest.
Revelation 2:6 (AMP)

---

[24] Romans 10:2
[25] 1 Corinthians 5:6

11

"I have this against you,
that you have left your first love."
Revelation 2:4

———⟶⟵———

DAY 4 ~ TEMPERATURE CHECK

The church in Ephesus received a strong commendation from our Lord, as we saw on Day 3. However, this toiling church that exposed false teachers who would attempt to lead her astray had a severe problem. One that Jesus warned, *I am coming to you and will remove your lampstand out of its place — unless you repent.'*[26]

Our opening verse reveals the actual condition of that fellowship. They had *left their first love*. What a heart-wrenching indictment. One that, if not corrected, comes with great consequence.

If we turn back the clock just thirty years before the book of Revelation, we read Paul's final words to that Ephesian church, which he planted. *Grace be with all those who love our Lord Jesus Christ with incorruptible love.*[27]

At the time of Paul's epistle, the Ephesian church exuded enthusiastic love toward our Lord. Love for Him naturally flowed in abundance as they fulfilled the greatest

[26] Revelation 2:5
[27] Ephesians 6:24

13

commandment.

A lawyer, asked (Jesus) a question, testing Him, "Teacher, which is the great commandment in the Law?"
And He said to him," 'YOU SHALL LOVE THE LORD YOUR GOD WITH ALL YOUR HEART, AND WITH ALL YOUR SOUL, AND WITH ALL YOUR MIND.' This is the great and foremost commandment."[28]

Though the church in Ephesus was busy with deeds and zealous to expose false teachers, they had lost sight of the reason for their toil. While these deeds deserved commendation, their motive for doing them was not based upon a deep, growing love for the Lord. This assembly had once loved Christ to such a degree that, their deeds flowing as an expression of it, the Apostle Paul could not help but mention it in his epistle. Yet, in thirty short years, they were simply going through the motions.

In Revelation 2:5, Jesus instructed the Ephesian church as to what would fix their lost love. *"Therefore remember from where you have fallen, and repent and do the deeds you did at first."* The suggestion was not that they needed to increase their deeds but to go back to their original motivation for doing them in

---

[28] Matthew 22:35-38

the first place—a genuine heart, soul, and mind love for God. They were to 1) Remember. 2) Repent. 3) Do deeds that reflected their love for Him.

Jesus' warning instructs us all. The consequence for that assembly is just as severe for us today. We must take time to consider what we do in Jesus' name. If our deeds are to us no more than cold duty, we must remember the zeal we had for Him at the beginning of our walk with Him. If coldness has set in, and we've forgotten that He is the object of our toil. In that case, we must confess, repent, and then follow Jesus in service with the same heart of joy, love, zeal, gratitude, and surrender we had for Him when we first came to trust, believe, and receive Him and His way to our salvation.

We become distracted and busy with so many "good deeds" that we can unwittingly accomplish them from a place of cold duty as we go through the motions. When and if this happens, Jesus calls us to repentance. I pray that my service to Him will always result from an overflow of my love for Him. How about you, have you checked your temperature lately?

"To him who overcomes, I will grant to eat of the tree of life which is in the Paradise of God."
Revelation 2:7

"Do not fear what you are about to suffer."
Revelation 2:10

———— ⬥ ————

DAY 5 ~ FAITHFULLY FACING FIRE

A t the time John wrote the words of our Lord to the seven churches noted in Revelation, Polycarp, who was a direct disciple of the Apostle John, was the Bishop at the church of Smyrna, the second assembly to be addressed. Though the congregants were materially impoverished, they were wealthy beyond measure in spiritual blessings. A far better wealth since Jesus taught us that He would prepare a place for us grander than we could ever imagine building during our short lifetime here on earth.[29] Regarding the riches of wisdom alone, His Word tells us that:

THINGS WHICH EYE HAS NOT SEEN AND EAR HAS NOT HEARD, AND which HAVE NOT ENTERED THE HEART OF MAN, ALL THAT GOD HAS PREPARED FOR THOSE WHO LOVE HIM."[30]

Smyrna looked forward to the reality of *"treasures in heaven, where neither moth nor*

---

[29] John 14:2-3
[30] Corinthians 2:9

rust destroys, and where thieves do not break in or steal."[31]

The assembly at Smyrna could boldly stand and proclaim to one another:

> Blessed be the God and Father of our Lord Jesus Christ, who according to His great mercy has caused us to be born again to a living hope through the resurrection of Jesus Christ from the dead, to obtain an inheritance which is imperishable and undefiled and will not fade away, reserved in heaven for you, who are protected by the power of God through faith for a salvation ready to be revealed in the last time.[32]

The church at Smyrna would suffer tribulation with a time limit. Not all would experience it in the same manner or to the point of martyrdom. Jesus' counsel to Smyrna? Be fearless in the face of what they would endure. This spiritually wealthy fellowship was armed with the Word of God, the knowledge of His promises, and the strength of the Holy Spirit within them. Therefore, when it came time for an aged and beloved Polycarp to face the flames, based on the knowledge and reality

---

[31] Matthew 6:20
[32] 1 Peter 1:3-5

of his living Savior, he accomplished that with awe-inspiring confidence.

"Swear," urged the Proconsul (of the Roman Empire to Polycarp who refused to sacrifice to their gods), "reproach Christ, and I will set you free."

"86 years have I served him," Polycarp declared, "and he has done me no wrong. How can I blaspheme my King and my Savior?

"You threaten me with fire which burns for an hour, and is then extinguished, but you know nothing of the fire of the coming judgment and eternal punishment, reserved for the ungodly. Why are you waiting? Bring on whatever you want."[33]

Jesus said, *"In the world you have tribulation, but take courage; I have overcome the world."*[34] He also reminded us that:

"If the world hates you, you know that it has hated Me before it hated you. If you were of the world, the world would love its own; but because you are not of the world, but I chose you out of the world, because of this the world hates you. Remember the word that I said to you, 'A

---

[33] https://christianhistoryinstitute.org/study/module/polycarp
[34] John 16:33

slave is not greater than his master.' If they persecuted Me, they will also persecute you; if they kept My word, they will keep yours also."[35]

Is the thought of persecution and possible martyrdom an image so far from your mind that you have never prayed to the Lord to help you face it? Does the current cultural climate trend toward a possibility in the future? Here in the United States, we should never assume that we are beyond the persecutions our brothers and sisters in other parts of the world endure. Hostility toward Christ and those who love Him is on the rise. Can you withstand as Polycarp? Or, would *go along to get along* be your anthem? Pray about these things. It might happen sooner than you ever imagined.

Thankfully, what awaits us is beyond comprehension, and no one and nothing will ever snatch our eternal reward from us. Fear not, because if or when the time comes for us to face persecution, be sure Jesus will give us the grace, strength, confidence, and power of the Holy Spirit to endure it all.

Be faithful until death,
and I will give you the crown of life.
Revelation 2:10

---

[35] John 15:18

"You hold fast My name,
and did not deny My faith."
Revelation 2:13

———— ⌖ ————

DAY 6 ~ WE SHALL OVERCOME

When considering the church at Pergamum, we cannot help but imagine an incredibly, stiflingly spiritually oppressive place as we read Jesus' words to the faithful believers located there.

> "I know where you dwell, where Satan's throne is; and you hold fast My name, and did not deny My faith even in the days of Antipas, My witness, My faithful one, who was killed among you, where Satan dwells."[36]

I believe that this is proof that we can proclaim the Gospel with power, even in the worst places. This makes it possible to live an uncompromising life, just as those whom Jesus commends and who are our focus for today.

We know nothing about Antipas beyond the above mentioned in Revelation. Though one

---

[36] Revelation 2:13

thing is sure, the faithful believers in the Pergamum assembly witnessed his martyrdom and were not opposed to facing it themselves if need be. They would not deny Christ as many others would on an annual basis.

In the city of Pergamum within a large yearly procession included, unfortunately, many professing believers. Incense was burned there on an altar dedicated to Zeus. As incense burned on that enormous altar, each individual proclaimed that Caesar was god while many professing believers would be forced to renounce Christ. The cults and the occult have one thing in common. They all deny the deity of Christ.

To renounce Jesus is to deny His attributes and character as God. For those professing believers in Pergamum, a false proclamation to Caesar and a public denial of Christ with an inward insincerity would provide momentary peace in the place where Satan dwelt. The pressure to refrain from going through the motions was simply too great. However, others stood firm and refused to deny Him.

In Matthew 10:32-33, Jesus said, *"Everyone who confesses Me before men, I will also confess him before My Father who is in heaven. But whoever denies Me before men, I will also deny him before My Father who is in heaven.* "

The Apostle John made clear the source of the denial in one of his epistles as we read:

> Who is the liar but the one who denies that Jesus is the Christ? This is the antichrist, the one who denies the Father and the Son.[37]

Many people today have private faith but make zero public professions of Christ. They are afraid of the same consequences as a Polycarp, or an Antipas suffered. Facing persecution for publicly professing the deity of Christ and our faith in Him can pose its hazards. However, to deny Him has weightier consequences.

Remember, as you go about the Father's business, sharing and proclaiming Christ, He sees and is pleased, especially if it happens to be in those less than friendly environments. No matter how much anyone turns up the heat, one thing is true; we can and shall overcome!

"To him who overcomes, to him I will give some of the hidden manna, and I will give him a white stone, and a new name written on the stone which no one knows but he who receives it."
Revelation 2:17

---

[37] 1 John 2:22

"I have a few things against you."
Revelation 2:14

DAY 7 ~ THE WAY TO REVIVAL

Where the Ephesian church diligently escorted the false teachers out of their back door; Pergamum allowed teachers who held to *the teaching of Balaam*[38] through their front door. They also tolerated those who held to *the teaching of the Nicolaitans.*[39]

Balaam, a soothsayer of Mesopotamia who was tempted by wealth, was prevented from cursing the children of Israel as King Balak desired. Balaam knew, however, that tripping them up by way of compromise through intermarrying, pagan worship, and sexual sin would bring about their fall and his payday.[40]

Balaam compromised for personal gain. It appears this might have been the same for some of those individuals in the assembly at Pergamum. Since, as we learned from Day 6, some in that fellowship felt it was better to go with the pagan flow than to exchange their comfortable lives with persecution or death.

Unfortunately, we can also have the same

---

[38] Revelation 2:14
[39] Revelation 2:15
[40] Numbers 22-24

mindset. So often, we remain silent as we tolerate *words from God* that someone states were given to him or her, but those *words* might be off, even slightly, from the Scriptural mark. This subtlety can lead folks to follow a person rather than Christ and the Scripturally ignorant away from the accurate Word of God.

On the other hand, perhaps we know of folks involved in perpetual compromise, but we remain silent since confronting them is an uncomfortable thing to do. Maybe they lead a ministry we would like to join, and a confrontation, no matter how loving, might risk the opportunity to teach there as well.

Peter warned us of the outcome when sin in the camp receives a wink and a nod. *Many will follow their sensuality, and because of them the way of the truth will be maligned.*[41]

What are we to do in the face of a *Balaam* or a said faith *Nicolaitan*?

Beloved, do not believe every spirit, but test the spirits to see whether they are from God, because many false prophets have gone out into the world.[42]

Somehow, regardless of this, we seem to justify much of what we hear and see with an array of colorful excuses as to why we can't *rock the boat* or leave if the leadership in the

---

[41] 2 Peter 2
[42] 1 John 4:1-3

fellowship will not return to the sound teaching of God's Word. Do any of the following justifications sound familiar to you?

"The worship is great! I just feel so blessed."

"I like the activities they have for kids and teens. All their friends go here."

"Everyone is so loving and accepting."

"The number of people is growing so much my pastor's now on television!"

"The service times work out well for my family and me."

"My family has been attending this church ever since I was a little kid!"

"I have a business, and it's never grown so big as when I started going here."

Pergamum was filled with false Christians. You might ask, is that possible? Yes. I was one of them. Not in Pergamum, but I had professed I was a born-again Christian for ten years, yet I was as lost as a rock. I was one to whom Jesus would have said, *"I never knew you; depart from Me, you who act wickedly [disregarding My commands]."*[43] All that changed in 1991 when I truly gave Him my life. Oh, what a difference He has meant in my life and for my soul.

Do you see compromise, or worse, are you

---

[43] Matthew 7:23 (AMP)

engaged in it, attempting to dismiss it by all the wonderful things you do in our Lord's name? We need to take to heart the words of Samuel, which could lead to revival if applied.

"Has the Lord as much delight in burnt offerings and sacrifices as in obeying the voice of the Lord? Behold, to obey is better than sacrifice, and to heed than the fat of rams. For rebellion is as the sin of divination, and insubordination is as iniquity and idolatry."[44]

In Pergamum, true believers who had fallen into corrupted teaching, or tolerated it, had an opportunity to repent. It is clear from the passage that our Lord wants us to deal with false teachers and Christian imposters. Since we are close to Christ's return, certainly closer than we were twenty-one-hundred years ago, now is the time to let your concerns be known with love. We owe that to Jesus and each other.

"To him who overcomes,
to him I will give some of the hidden manna,
and I will give him a white stone,
and a new name written on the stone
which no one knows but he who receives it."
Revelation 2:17

---

[44] 1 Samuel 15:22-23

"I know your deeds, and your love and faith and service and perseverance, and that your deeds of late are greater than at first."
Revelation 2:19

———— ❧ ————

DAY 8 ~ THE FAB FIVE

As we read Jesus' message to the church in Thyatira, the description of Him is a mighty one and consistent with John's in Revelation 1. Jesus had *eyes like a flame of fire*, allowing us the image of an intense examination of that fellowship, assuring the reader that *there is no creature hidden from His sight, but all things are open and laid bare to the eyes of Him with whom we have to do.*[45]

The description continues as Jesus depicts His *feet like burnished bronze*, another simile, and this time communicating His strength, stability, and justice as we read in Revelation 19:15.

The passages above are also consistent with Daniel's description below:

I lifted my eyes and looked, and behold, there was a certain man dressed in linen, whose waist was girded with a belt of pure gold of Uphaz. His body also was like beryl, his face had the appearance of

---
[45] Hebrews 4:13

lightning, his eyes were like flaming torches, his arms and feet like the gleam of polished bronze, and the sound of his words like the sound of a tumult.[46]

Since all things and people are open and laid bare before Him, Jesus understands the circumstances we face. Especially since *we do not have a high priest who cannot sympathize with our weaknesses, but One who has been tempted in all things as we are, yet without sin.*[47]

On an intimate level, Jesus realizes how difficult it is to live among a depraved and pagan culture, having had to cast out demons and encountered Satan in the wilderness.

In His commendation, Jesus found some believers in the church of Thyatira to have had the following:

    1) Love
    2) Faith
    3) Service
    4) Perseverance
    5) Later deeds greater than at first [48]

Regarding the first point, the Apostle Paul wrote, *If I speak with the tongues of men and of angels, but do not have love, I have become a*

---

[46] Daniel 10:5-6
[47] Hebrews 4:15
[48] Revelation 2:19

noisy gong or a clanging cymbal.[49] When our love for others is not palpable, our speech becomes to them as making noise.

The particular believers addressed in the church of Thyatira displayed love to those of the fellowship, those they served, and toward God Himself.

Regarding faith, we find the importance of this with what Paul cautioned Titus. Referring to overseers, Paul said they should be *holding fast the faithful word which is in accordance with the teaching, so that he will be able both to exhort in sound doctrine and to refute those who contradict.*[50]

The faithful in Thyatira were true to the Lord and His Word. Their service was devoted and with the right motives and perseverance. We find in Revelation 14:12 a proper definition. *Here is the perseverance of the saints who keep the commandments of God and their faith in Jesus.*

By abiding in Christ, expressing genuine love, faith, service, and perseverance, it naturally flowed that the deeds of some believers in Thyatira would be greater than when they first came to know Him.

These particular believers in Thyatira had works that sprang from their love for Christ. They were not serving to oppress others or in an attempt to earn their way into God's good

---

[49] 1 Corinthians 13:1
[50] Titus 1:9

graces. Those exceptional individuals who received Jesus' commendation would bear up under the load of living with paganism surrounding them.

How precious that our Lord examines so personally and so thoroughly the works we do, our motives, and then commends us when we stand firm in the faith.

Love, faith, service, perseverance, and a growing level of commitment, which results in a greater quantity and quality of deeds in His Name, will be the mark of the mature believer.

Examine that list and see if you lack in any area. If so, pray that the Lord will show you how to reverse that trend. Since I have to review that list often, I suspect we already know before we ask. Lift it to Him today, make the necessary adjustments, and hold fast until He comes.

"But I say to you,
the rest who are in Thyatira—
I place no other burden on you.
Nevertheless what you have,
hold fast until I come."
Revelation 2:24-25

"You tolerate the woman Jezebel, who calls herself a prophetess, and she teaches and leads My bond-servants astray so that they commit acts of immorality and eat things sacrificed to idols."
Revelation 2:20

DAY 9 ~ AMERICA'S ALTER

Thyatira was a central hub for trade guilds or unions. An essential aspect of being a member, which allowed you to engage in employment or trade, was the requirement to participate in pagan feasts. Participants paid homage to particular gods or goddesses that represented the various trades. In Thyatira, professing believers also attended as they ate the meat sacrificed to idols and engaged in sexual immorality.

At the church in Thyatira, the behavior at these pagan feasts was condoned and encouraged by a self-appointed prophetess, whom our Lord referred to as *Jezebel.*

If you conduct a word study on *Jezebel* throughout the Scriptures, you will understand what a wicked person she was. Jezebel was so corrupt that her name has become synonymous with paganism, fornication, and abject evil.

Thyatira's *Jezebel* seduced believers by her teaching to lead them into cultural and sexual compromise and eventually paganism. Her *children*, referred to in Jesus' letter, followed her in her immoral teachings and practice.

Is it possible that the United States of America has also fallen for the teaching of our own homegrown *Jezebel*? Was there a twentieth-century *Jezebel* whose influence has bled into this, the twenty-first century? Consider her words:

> "The most merciful thing that the large family does to one of its infant members is to kill it."[51]

> "... these two words [birth control] sum up our whole philosophy... It means the release and cultivation of the better elements in our society, and the gradual suppression, elimination, and eventual extinction, of defective stocks -- those human weeds which threaten the blooming of the finest flowers of American civilization."[52]

In an interview with Mike Wallace in 1957, this modern-day racist, eugenicist, and *Jezebel* could not say whether infidelity was a sin.

---

[51] *Woman and the New Race*, Chapter 5, "The Wickedness of Creating Large Families." (1920) http://www.bartleby.com/1013/
[52] Margaret Sanger, "High Lights in the History of Birth Control," Oct 1923. https://www.nyu.edu/projects/s...

However, she had a definite opinion on what was:

"I think the greatest sin in the world is bringing children into the world, that have disease from their parents, that have no chance in the world to be a human being practically... Delinquents, prisoners, all sorts of things just marked when they're born. That to me is the greatest sin—that people can—can commit."[53]

Margaret Sanger, who expressed those horrendous and disgusting thoughts above and so much more, was the founder of Planned Parenthood.

I often wonder what the reaction would be in the United States of America if we witnessed tens of millions of babies as they were sacrificed on alters publicly throughout our major cities, rather than privately in a clinic so-called. Would there be an outcry?

Through the legalization of abortion and the organization she founded, our modern-day *Jezebel* has allowed many individuals, even in our churches, to condone the extinguishing of

---

[53] https://www.youtube.com/watch?v=CrkrkSiFApA

scores of fellow Image-Bearers. It has become easy for people to live in sexual sin and gain a cover for sexual assault, eliminating the evidence through this ultimate form of child abuse.

Abortion, a word that causes us to bristle when we hear it, not only destroys lives, it damages women in ways incalculable—heart, soul, and mind; women who need our love and guidance. Abortion is not the unforgivable sin, but repentance, and after that, healing is possible, as countless women can proclaim.

However, what will our Lord do to an unrepentant nation? There is still time to repent and stand up and speak out. Can you commit to making an impact before it's too late? God help us if we refuse.

"Behold, I will throw her on a bed of sickness, and those who commit adultery with her into great tribulation, unless they repent of her deeds. And I will kill her children with pestilence, and all the churches will know that I am He who searches the minds and hearts; and I will give to each one of you according to your deeds."
Revelation 2:22-23

*"You have a few people in Sardis
who have not soiled their garments;
and they will walk with Me in white,
for they are worthy."*

Revelation 3:4

DAY 10 ~ THE FAITHFUL FEW

Christianity is not a numbers game. The goal should not be to pack the pews to the point where the congregation needs ten service times per Sunday. Quality is far more critical to our Lord than quantity, as Jesus cautioned us to:

> "Enter through the narrow gate; for the gate is wide and the way is broad that leads to destruction, and there are many who enter through it. For the gate is small and the way is narrow that leads to life, and there are few who find it."[54]

According to our Lord's letter to them in Revelation 3, the church at Sardis was an assembly that had made a name for themselves in that prominent city. Sardis was indeed

---

[54] Matthew 7:13-14

famous but in *their* name only as Jesus understood the extent, quality, quantity, and motivation behind their works. Unfortunately, He determined their results as *dead*, and even the remainder was *about to die*.[55]

However, Jesus also found a *few people* of the church in Sardis who kept their love and passion for Him alive. They did not stain their garments by the apathy and hypocrisy surrounding them in that assembly. They were also unsoiled from the corrupt environment in which they lived since Sardis was home to one of the seven largest pagan temples dedicated to Artemis.

To these *few people* at Sardis, Jesus granted a particular word of commendation. This we should find very encouraging. No matter where we are, no matter the difficulty, even if there are only a few of us remaining faithful, He knows all about it, and He will reward us if we continue in perseverance. These faithful few were not phonies. They were not apathetic. They continued to *contend earnestly for the faith which was once for all handed down to the saints.*[56] They bloomed where God planted them, and He commended them for it.

A few can make a huge impact. The disciples were only a *few people*, yet they turned the

---

[55] Revelation 3:1-2
[56] Jude 3

world upside down, or rather right side up, for whoever received the Gospel.

To the few faithful believers in Sardis, Christ's reward to them was to walk side by side with Him in white. In Revelation 7, we realize the significance of being clothed in white:

> After these things I looked, and behold, a great multitude which no one could count, from every nation and all tribes and peoples and tongues, standing before the throne and before the Lamb, clothed in white robes, and palm branches were in their hands; and they cry out with a loud voice, saying, "Salvation to our God who sits on the throne, and to the Lamb."[57]
>
> "These are the ones who come out of the great tribulation, and they have washed their robes and made them white in the blood of the Lamb."[58]

It is a fantastic thing to imagine that washing a robe in blood could make it white. However, that is what happened to our sin when The Lamb of God washed it in the blood He shed through His suffering and death on the cross. Consider the following three passages:

> "For the life of the flesh is in the blood, and I have given it to you on the altar to

---

[57] Revelation 7:9-10
[58] Revelation 7:14

make atonement for your souls; for it is the blood by reason of the life that makes atonement."[59]

And according to the Law, one may almost say, all things are cleansed with blood, and without shedding of blood there is no forgiveness.[60]

"Come now, and let us reason together," Says the Lord, "Though your sins are as scarlet, They will be as white as snow; Though they are red like crimson, They will be like wool."[61]

Those *few people* in Sardis walked worthy and remained consistent, keeping themselves untainted by the polluted environment surrounding them within the fellowship and without. This is not an easy thing to do. However, the few in Sardis certainly gives us hope. If they did it, by the power of the Holy Spirit, we can also and expect to stroll with Jesus in Glory wearing garments given to us by Him—clean, bright, and as white as snow.

"He who overcomes will thus be clothed in white garments; and I will not erase his name from the book of life, and I will confess his name before My Father and before His angels."
Revelation 3:5

---

[59] Leviticus 17:11
[60] Hebrews 9:22
[61] Isaiah 1:18

"You have a name that you are alive,
but you are dead."
Revelation 3:1

DAY 11 ~ AN UNHEALTHY MASK

As we learned from Day 10, and from our Lord's words in the sad indictment above, the church at Sardis was one in name only. They might have had a name that impressed others, but behind closed doors, Sardis was a fellowship that suffered from the sin of hypocrisy, one of the main obstacles that unbelievers will hurl at the believer who attempts to witness to them. They were *holding to a form of godliness, although they have denied its power.*[62]

Hypocrisy in the church, defined as *wearing a mask*, is not a reflection on Christ but upon our fallen nature and genuine need for Him. A plastic smile might look good to others in the congregation, but it can only be maintained long enough to accommodate the length of a church service. When the individual goes home, their family lives the ugly truth. Do we think others do not see through that? He who has

---

[62] 2 Timothy 3:5

eyes as a flame of fire sure does.

How does this happen? How does someone who was once on fire for the Lord fall into hypocrisy and dead deeds? Our Lord revealed the answer to Sardis and many others in the same condition.

Sardis had fallen asleep. They were not watchful and thus were inattentive to their spiritual decline, and as the deadness settled in, they simply went through the motions.

Revelation 3 is not the only time we find our Lord admonishing His followers to be awake, alert, and to watch out.

> "The eye is the lamp of your body; when your eye is clear, your whole body also is full of light; but when it is bad, your body also is full of darkness. Then watch out that the light in you is not darkness."[63]

If we close our eyes to the Gospel or put things before our eyes that dim the light within us, darkness will fill those areas and eventually overtake us if we are not watchful.

Jesus warned:

> "Watch out and beware of the leaven

---

[63] Luke 11:34-35

of the Pharisees and Sadducees."

They understood that He did not say to beware of the leaven of bread, but of the teaching of the Pharisees and Sadducees. [64]

Seven times in Matthew 23, the Lord stated, *"Woe to you, scribes and Pharisees, hypocrites,"* before giving them a stunning rebuke. Their overarching concern with ritual, performance, and status gained them the title of *hypocrite*. Their *service* was not for God but for elevating themselves, as they loved to be called by their title. Unfortunately, what the scribes, Pharisees, and Sadducees produced was the epitome of dead works.

Sleeping when it is crucial to be watchful was not confined to Sardis. Consider the sleepy Apostles in the Garden of Gethsemane:

"So, you men could not keep watch with Me for one hour? Keep watching and praying that you may not enter into temptation; the spirit is willing, but the flesh is weak."[65]

The above hits home for us all—willing yet weak flesh. Satan has a target on our back as Peter, who knew from experience, reminded his readers to *be of sober spirit, be on the alert.*

---

[64] Matthew 16:6, 12
[65] Matthew 26:40-41

Your adversary, the devil, prowls around like a roaring lion, seeking someone to devour.[66]

The priority we place on entertaining ourselves is tragic. We have many opportunities and devices for escape. When we are not watchful, we can become drowsy, which leads to self-indulgence, hypocrisy, and dead deeds.

When we are distracted and drowsy, it is tough to be watchful. Sometimes we need to go back to the fundamentals of the faith, dive into His Word, and remember all that Jesus saved us from and for what purpose. It certainly was not to continually hit the snooze button. Therefore, wake up, watch, and remember all the blessings He lavishes upon you and serve Him once again with the original love and zeal you had when you first gave Him your life.

"So remember what you have received and heard; and keep it, and repent.
Therefore if you do not wake up,
I will come like a thief, and you will not know at what hour I will come to you."
Revelation 3:3

---

[66] 1 Peter 5:8

*"I know your deeds. Behold, I have put before
you an open door which no one can shut,
because you have a little power, and have kept
My word, and have not denied My name."*
Revelation 3:8

———— ⌒✦⌒ ————

DAY 12 ~ LITTLE POWER, BIG LOVE

I n His letter to them, Christ gave no rebuke
to the church of Philadelphia. It seemed
appropriate that this fellowship would be
located in a city that, when translated, means
Brotherly Love though named well before the
birth of Christ and proclamation of the Gospel.
The Philadelphian church was a fellowship with
little power but lots of love.

The Philadelphian believers were a beautiful
picture of the Christian walk in right standing.
These were believers who did not move in their
strength but were *strong in the Lord and in the
strength of His might.*[67] Whatever strength
Philadelphia would have would come from the
Lord. If we are dependent upon His strength
and power, though we have little to none of
our own, His is enough.

The church at Philadelphia was also faithful

---

[67] Ephesians 6:10

to the Word of God. They trusted it, knew it, and lived it. They read it and applied it as God the Holy Spirit had communicated it through those who penned it, and thus Jesus commended them.

So too, the Philadelphian church was wholly devoted to Jesus Christ and the Father who sent Him. They would not deny their relationship with Christ, His deity, the fact of His resurrection, and His soon return.

When we consider Christ's words to them, the Philadelphian fellowship is a beautiful example to all believers. They were grounded in the basics of the Faith and expressed it with love and humility. If we could have those same characteristics, oh, how the Lord would use us to influence a world that senses things are not right and time as fleeting.

If those in Philadelphia, the *City of Brotherly Love*, were going to have an *open door*, they could not be ashamed of Him or His Gospel. Their love would overflow with a desire to reach others for Christ. The Apostle Paul said:

> For I am not ashamed of the gospel, for it is the power of God for salvation to everyone who believes, to the Jew first

and also to the Greek.[68]

What a testimony. Do you love others enough to tell them about the Lord regardless of outward appearances or intimidations? Could this be why we do not find ourselves in a *City of Brotherly Love* but in a culture of mean?

This present world needs us to love them enough and be faithful to our Lord and His Word so that we *may proclaim the excellencies of Him who has called* (us) *out of darkness into His marvelous light.*[69]

What about loving those who are not easy to love and who perpetuate the culture of mean? Astonishingly, Jesus words to those who spat at Him, beat Him, mocked Him, betrayed Him, abandoned Him, rejected Him, crucified Him, and gambled at the foot of His cross for His garments were:

"Father, forgive them; for they do not know what they are doing."[70]

Jesus gave His life, the ultimate sign of love, for others—even for those who reviled, tortured and hated Him.

[68] Romans 1:16
[69] 1 Peter 2:9
[70] Luke 23:34

Believers in Philadelphia took their eyes off themselves and looked at those who oppressed them through the eyes of Jesus. When we imitate a church like Philadelphia or our Lord, we no longer feel anger toward them because we realize that:

> Our struggle is not against flesh and blood, but against the rulers, against the powers, against the world forces of this darkness, against the spiritual forces of wickedness in the heavenly places.[71]

The opposition we face is not from an individual when attacked because of our faith. They are simply a pawn. This is why we love the individual but are not too thrilled about how they treat us. However, by our love for them, we can win them over. They might not be our brother or sister in Christ; however, they are in Adam. Will you commit to reaching a lost world with brotherly love as Philadelphia? It is what Christ commands and commends.

"I am coming quickly; hold fast what you have, so that no one will take your crown."
Revelation 3:11

---

[71] Ephesians 6:12

"He who is holy, who is true, who has the key of David, who opens and no one will shut, and who shuts and no one opens."
Revelation 3:7

———— ❧ ————

DAY 13 ~ THE KEY TO REVIVAL

What of this key? The words of our Lord above to the church at Philadelphia prompt us to study further. As we search the Scriptures, we find a prophecy in Isaiah concerning Eliakim who would replace a *contemptible steward and treasurer* named Shebna, a man who was *in charge of the royal household*, and was more about *his* glory than the Lord's:

"Then it will come about in that day, that I will summon My servant Eliakim the son of Hilkiah, and I will clothe him with your tunic and tie your sash securely about him. I will entrust him with your authority, and he will become a father to the inhabitants of Jerusalem and to the house of Judah.

"Then I will set the key of the house of David on his shoulder, when he opens no one will shut, when he shuts no one will open. I will drive him like a peg in a firm place, and he will become a throne of glory to his father's house.

"So they will hang on him all the glory of his father's house, offspring and issue, all the least of vessels, from bowls to all the jars.

"In that day," declares the Lord of hosts, "the peg driven in a firm place will give way; it will even break off and fall, and the load hanging on it will be cut off, for the Lord has spoken."[72]

The Isaiah passages above apply to Eliakim and double as a Messianic prophecy. From the last paragraph above, it is also a picture of the cross.

As we continue in the Scriptures, we find Peter, when asked by Jesus who he believed Jesus was, did not hesitate to proclaim, *"You are the Christ, the Son of the living God."*[73] Jesus' response was a great gift given, not only to Peter but also to all who profess His name and identity.

"Blessed are you, Simon Barjona, because flesh and blood did not reveal this to you, but My Father who is in heaven. I also say to you that you are Peter, and upon this rock I will build My church; and the gates of Hades will not overpower it.

"I will give you the keys of the kingdom

---

[72] Isaiah 22:20-25
[73] Matthew 16:16

of heaven; and whatever you bind on earth shall have been bound in heaven, and whatever you loose on earth shall have been loosed in heaven."[74]

As do we who share Christ with others, Peter would have the ability to proclaim sins retained or forgiven based upon their willingness to believe and receive the Lord Jesus Christ and His way for the redemption of their soul. Peter was blessed with many opportunities to step through open doors and proclaim this to others.

Paul stated in 1 Corinthians 16:9, *A wide door for effective service has opened to me, and there are many adversaries.* In 2 Corinthians 2:12, he wrote that when he *came to Troas for the gospel of Christ* that *a door was opened for me in the Lord.*

In Colossians 4:3, Paul admonished us to pray *that God will open up to us a door for the word, so that we may speak forth the mystery of Christ.*

Luke stated in Acts 14:27, concerning the missionary journeys of Paul and Barnabas, that *when they had arrived and gathered the church together, they began to report all things that God had done with them and how He had opened a door of faith to the Gentiles.*

In light of the above passages, one thing is

---

[74] Matthew 16:17-19

certain; the key originates with Jesus Christ. He is the One Who ultimately holds the key and places it in the proper lock.

The Lord is the One Who opens the door of our hearts and opportunities, and we should step through while those doors remain open to the Gospel.

Philadelphia had an open door that the Lord said no one would be able to shut. Paul had an open door as well, and with it came *many adversaries*. An open door does not mean all is going to be smooth sailing.

We have had adversaries since the garden. Satan did not beguile Eve because he was on her side. I believe the Lord will open doors for us as well. However, will we, despite *many adversaries*, like Paul eagerly step through them? Perhaps the key He turns for you just might unlock the door that leads to using you for a radical revival.

"Do not be afraid; I am the first and the last, and the living One; and I was dead, and behold, I am alive forevermore, and I have the keys of death and of Hades."
Revelation 1:17-18

"I am rich, and have become wealthy, and have need of nothing,"
Revelation 3:17

―――――⌒⌒――――――

DAY 14 ~ LULLED INTO LAODICEA

The church in Laodicea was the last of the seven recipients of a letter from our Lord. After reviewing Revelation 3:14-22, you cannot help but notice that they did not receive any commendation, unlike the other churches. That alone should give us pause. However, there are aspects regarding this community that shed light upon Jesus' powerful words.

The water, attained through their limestone aqueduct system from a neighboring hot spring, was lukewarm and bitter by the time it reached Laodicea. One sip of the awful bitterness would cause you to spit as soon as it hit your taste buds. It did not quench thirst, and since it was lukewarm, it was neither hot enough for bathing nor cool enough to refresh on a hot day. Thus, the final product of their limestone aqueduct was inadequate for use.

While unsuccessful in attaining pure and refreshing drinking water, the people of

Laodicea were successful in other ways. After suffering a catastrophic earthquake in AD 60, they financed the entire rebuilding relying solely upon their vast wealth. They attained zero assistance from Rome.

Aiding in their financial success, located in Laodicea, was a medical school where they manufactured a particular eye salve, which they boasted could cure most eye diseases. People traveled long distances to attain the cure.

The city of Laodicea was also famous for its unique textiles. They made clothing, special rugs, and other materials from ultra-soft and beautiful black wool. Roman royalty and many others would travel long distances for these materials, adding to their great wealth.

Therefore, the people in the church at Laodicea were financially self-sufficient, clothed like royalty, and should they succumb to the risk of an eye infection, a short trip to their medical school removed that burden as well. However, it is to this self-sufficient, self-reliant, and self-consumed congregation in Laodicea that Jesus communicated His most scathing rebuke.

It is interesting to note, in our self-sufficiency, how we can forget Jesus' attributes and character. However, perhaps we can add to what I outlined in Day 2 of this resource, how he described Himself in introducing His letter to Laodicea.

He is the *Amen*. He is unchangeable, the *I AM*.[75] *Jesus Christ is the same yesterday and today and forever*.[76] In 2 Corinthians 1:20, Jesus is the final word and authority as we read:

> For as many as are the promises of God, in Him they are yes; therefore also through Him is our Amen to the glory of God through us.

As the *faithful and true Witness*, it is to Him we turn for every need, answer, and direction. He is faithful to respond to our petitions with either *yes*, *no*, or *wait*.

> Therefore, those also who suffer according to the will of God shall entrust their souls to a faithful Creator in doing what is right.[77]

Lastly, in the description of Himself to the church in Laodicea, Jesus is *the Beginning of the creation of God.* Confirming the above passage that He was not created at the beginning; He is the Creator of all from *its* beginning.

---

[75] Exodus 3:14, John 8 :58
[76] Hebrews 13:8
[77] 1 Peter 4:19

All things came into being through Him, and apart from Him, nothing came into being that has come into being.[78]

He is the image of the invisible God, the firstborn of all creation. For by Him all things were created, both in the heavens and on earth, visible and invisible, whether thrones or dominions or rulers or authorities — all things have been created through Him and for Him.[79]

With Christ's description of Himself and Laodicea in mind, consider the opening verse and how many people boast likewise. Take time today to prepare your heart for tomorrow as we delve into His words to a church much like that in the United States of America and other affluent countries that profess Him.

An exchange from self-serving to self-examination would prove far better. It is easy for affluence and the pressure to succeed to lull us away from Jesus and into Laodicea. Can you relate?

"The Amen, the faithful and true Witness, the Beginning of the creation of God, says this: 'I know your deeds...'"
Revelation 3:14-15

---

[78] John 1:3
[79] Colossians 1:15-16

"You do not know that you are wretched and miserable and poor and blind and naked."
Revelation 3:17

DAY 15 ~ THE GREAT PHYSICIAN

One of the worst character flaws a person can possess is a lack of self-awareness, as it blinds you to what everyone else can see. Read the opening verse for Day 14, and then reread the above verse. It is quite a stark contrast.

Jesus, looking upon those at the church in Laodicea, saw through the trappings of their wealth, self-confidence, and self-reliance. What He saw were *wretched, miserable, poor, blind,* and *naked* people.

As Jesus knocked on the outside of the church's door in Laodicea, and the congregation enjoyed an atmosphere of fellowship inside, He communicated His stinging rebuke:

"I know your deeds, that you are neither cold nor hot; I wish that you were cold or hot. So because you are lukewarm, and neither hot nor cold, I will spit you out of My mouth."[80]

Just as a Laodicean who sipped the bitterly warm water that flowed from their limestone aqueduct system would spew it out, Jesus will do the same to those of that fellowship. This is an ultimate rejection. There is no hope for the apathetic or the spiritually indifferent.

For the hot and on fire for the Lord, you are useful for service. Nothing is beyond your ability if you put Jesus first in your life.

For the cold, those who know little to nothing about Jesus or spiritual matters, they are like blank slates with no preconceptions, making them more willing to *reason together* concerning the Gospel.[81]

However, what of the spiritually apathetic, indifferent, detached, disinterested, the lukewarm concerning Jesus Christ, who enter the fellowship believing they are saved because they walked through the door but left Jesus knocking on the outside? Their condition is far worse than spiritual laziness. Theirs is an arrogance that, when confronted, will defend themselves with their list of deeds—deeds which Jesus already knows.

---

[80] Revelation 3:15-16
[81] Isaiah 1:18

"Every tree that does not bear good fruit is cut down and thrown into the fire. So then, you will know them by their fruits.

"Not everyone who says to Me, 'Lord, Lord,' will enter the kingdom of heaven, but he who does the will of My Father who is in heaven will enter.

"Many will say to Me on that day, 'Lord, Lord, did we not prophesy in Your name, and in Your name cast out demons, and in Your name perform many miracles?' And then I will declare to them, 'I never knew you; DEPART FROM ME, YOU WHO PRACTICE LAWLESSNESS.'"[82]

Did you notice that Jesus did not say a few but that many will claim Him? Why is it easy for the lukewarm to be so blind? Because the lukewarm in our congregations are not alone. They can look condemningly at those who are cold because the lukewarm do just enough to wear the Christian facade. They can look at those who are hot and mutter to themselves that their zeal cannot be genuine. Tragically, their great blessings, instead of making them thankful, grateful, humble people who help

---

[82] Matthew 7:19-23

others, simply blinds and bankrupts them. Jesus' cure for the lukewarm condition is as follows:

> "I advise you to buy from Me gold refined by fire so that you may become rich, and white garments so that you may clothe yourself, and that the shame of your nakedness will not be revealed; and eye salve to anoint your eyes so that you may see. Those whom I love, I reprove and discipline; therefore be zealous and repent."[83]

Jesus, Himself alone, is our cure. Everything that great city boastfully possessed, and ours, Christ can supply and He is enough. If you feel the only time you ever connected with the Lord was the day of your conversion, perhaps you have been lulled into Laodicea. Respond and repent now. Can you sense the urgency? Pray Psalm 51 aloud, applying it to yourself. Do not delay. He is knocking at the door even now.

"He who has an ear, let him hear what the Spirit says to the churches."
Revelation 3:22

---

[83] Revelation 3:18-19

*"HOLY, HOLY, HOLY is THE LORD GOD,
THE ALMIGHTY, WHO WAS AND WHO IS
AND WHO IS TO COME."*
Revelation 4:8

------ ⟡ ------

DAY 16 ~ HALLOWED FATHER

The worshipful, impassioned words above were expressed from a place of abject awe and devotion. The Scriptures tell us that day and night these words do not cease around the throne of God. As addressed on Day 1, the Apostle John was an eyewitness to what he penned in the book of Revelation; therefore, his testimony, no matter how hard to understand or imagine, is sure. Although the image John saw of those who cried the words of our opening verse is astonishing, they pale in comparison to the vision of God the Father, Himself, seated upon His throne.

A throne was standing in heaven, and One sitting on the throne. And He who was sitting was like a jasper stone and a sardius in appearance; and there was a rainbow around the throne, like an emerald in appearance.[84]

The following is an account from the Prophet Isaiah, who was another eyewitness:

> I saw the Lord sitting on a throne, lofty and exalted, with the train of His robe filling the temple. Seraphim stood above Him, each having six wings: with two he covered his face, and with two he covered his feet, and with two he flew. And one called out to another and said, "Holy, Holy, Holy, is the Lord of hosts, The whole earth is full of His glory." And the foundations of the thresholds trembled at the voice of him who called out, while the temple was filling with smoke.[85]

Isaiah's response? *Then I said, "Woe is me, for I am ruined! Because I am a man of unclean lips, and I live among a people of unclean lips; for my eyes have seen the King, the Lord of hosts."*[86]
Isaiah was utterly *verklempt.* He was completely overcome with emotion, feeling unclean and unworthy, until a lump of burning coal touched his lips to purify him long enough to stand before God's throne.

In 2 Corinthians, the Apostle Paul stated:

---

[84] Revelation 4:2-3
[85] Isaiah 6:1-4
[86] Isaiah 6:5

I know a man in Christ who fourteen years ago—whether in the body I do not know, or out of the body I do not know, God knows—such a man was caught up to the third heaven. And I know how such a man—whether in the body or apart from the body I do not know, God knows— was caught up into Paradise and heard inexpressible words, which a man is not permitted to speak.[87]

Though Paul refrained from sharing the details, the humility with which he communicated his experience is enough.

Sometimes I wonder if the curtain between heaven and earth suddenly fell and we could see our Great God sitting upon His throne, what would be our reaction? No wonder, when Jesus taught us to pray, He instructed us to begin with, *"Our Father who is in heaven, Hallowed be Your name."*[88]

While God's name is *Hallowed*, Jesus also instructed us to refer to God as *Father*. This was an astonishing statement when He taught His disciples to pray and address God in such a manner, and I believe it still is.

It is an amazing thought to consider that this almighty, infinitely powerful Being, Whose voice makes everything tremble, we can refer to in such an intimate way—*Father*. How is this

---

[87] 2 Corinthians 12:2-4
[88] Matthew 6:9

possible? Paul explained:

But when the fullness of the time came, God sent forth His Son, born of a woman, born under the Law, so that He might redeem those who were under the Law, that we might receive the adoption as sons. Because you are sons, God has sent forth the Spirit of His Son into our hearts, crying, "Abba! Father!" Therefore you are no longer a slave, but a son; and if a son, then an heir through God.[89]

The above explanation is why, when life is hard, or we seek God's will, we may *draw near with confidence to the throne of grace*[90] all because Jesus made it possible for us to refer to God as *Father, my Father*. Therefore, we have a twofold purpose for falling before Him. We worship out of love for offering His only begotten Son as the price for our redemption and adoption, and because God our Father is *HOLY, HOLY, HOLY—LORD GOD, THE ALMIGHTY*.

"God thunders with His voice wondrously, Doing great things which we cannot comprehend."
Job 37:5

---

[89] Galatians 4:4-7
[90] Hebrews 4:16

"Worthy are You, our Lord and our God, to receive glory and honor and power; for You created all things, and because of Your will they existed, and were created."
Revelation 4:11

DAY 17 ~ "WHY AM I HERE?"

In light of the continual cry of *"HOLY, HOLY, HOLY is THE LORD GOD, THE ALMIGHTY, WHO WAS AND WHO IS AND WHO IS TO COME,"*[91] before the throne of God that we reflected upon for Day 16, we also have to consider what followed.

The Apostle John reported that others *fall prostrate before Him Who is sitting on the throne, and they worship Him Who lives forever and ever; and they throw down their crowns before the throne, crying out*[92] today's opening verse. As one group cried out regarding His holiness times three—Father, Son, and Holy Spirit—still others before the throne of God cried of His worthiness.

When I reflect upon our Lord's promises to overcoming believers—white garments,[93] a

---

[91] Revelation 4:8
[92] Revelation 4:10
[93] Revelation 3:5

65

crown,[94] sitting upon a throne[95]—it feels natural to relate to these who threw down their crowns at the foot of our Holy, Worthy, Almighty God. Though given to us by Him, our crown really belongs to Him for all He has done for us. He is worthy! More precious to us than the crown He places upon our brow will be a spontaneous prostration before Him in worship.

God alone is worthy of glory, honor, and power, not because *we* say so, but because of who He is. Because our God is the one, true, and living God, this means He is worthy on that basis alone. We simply have the opportunity to proclaim that fact. Therefore, God's worthiness does not rely upon human opinion. We merely recognize attributes that He already possesses.

As we break down our opening passage, we understand our worship is for God, the Creator of all things, including you and me. This is why creating an idol is foolish, as we find in Isaiah 44. As the process goes, folks will chop down a tree—one that God created—apply as much of it as possible toward utility, and then they *make the rest of it into an abomination*, and *fall down*

---

[94] Revelation 2:10, 3:11
[95] Revelations 3:21

before a block of wood![96] The foolishness of this seems magnified by the visual in our minds.

God is not only the Creator but also the *Sustainer* as well. He *upholds all things by the word of His power*[97] since *He is before all things, and in Him all things hold together.*[98] But oh, if He were ever to let go! We who stand nonchalantly on Earth as it spins at a rate of one thousand miles-per-hour never consider what would happen if He simply said, *"Stop!"* As the first and final cause of all things, by His word, He spoke the universe into existence, and He sustains it by the *word of His power* as well.

Then we come to the astonishing climax of the elder's cry before His throne. This is when we realize the reason for our existence. So many ask, *Why was I born?* or *Why did God bother to create me?* The answer is simple yet profound. The twenty-four elders who fell before God's throne stated that *because of Your will they existed, and were created."*[99]

God created us simply because He wanted to and not, as some have charged, because He was lonely. Nothing is lacking in God. He is very content with the fellowship within the Godhead as Father, Son, and Holy Spirit. God

---

[96] Isaiah 44:19
[97] Hebrews 1:3
[98] Colossians 1:17
[99] Revelation 4:11

created us because He wanted us, each one of us, as we find that *the Lord has made everything [to accommodate itself and contribute] to its own end and His own purpose —even the wicked [are fitted for their role] for the day of calamity and evil.*[100] If God has a purpose for the wicked, He has one for you too!

When you think of the extraordinary vision of God upon His throne and that He loves you, He wants what is best for you, including a love relationship with you that is almost too much for the human mind to comprehend.

By His will, He brought you and me into existence. Therefore, what is our responsibility to Him? How can we be lukewarm or apathetic? How can we ignore so great a God as our God?

We should also lie prostrate before God, crying out to Him the opening passage. What excellent practice as preparation for Glory. Consider doing this in a quiet and private place, listen for Him to speak to your soul, and then give Him the glory, worship, praise, and honor He is so due. He is worthy!

God created man in His own image, in the image of God He created him; male and female He created them. God blessed them.
Genesis 1:27-28

---

[100] Proverbs 16:4 (AMP)

"Worthy is the Lamb that was slain to receive power and riches and wisdom and might and honor and glory and blessing."
Revelation 5:12

DAY 18 ~ MEANT FOR EVIL

John, our eyewitness at the throne of God in Revelation 5, saw and *heard the voice of many angels around the throne and the living creatures and the elders; and the number of them was myriads of myriads, and thousands of thousands, saying with a loud voice*[101] the great proclamation in today's verse above.

Who is the Lamb *that was slain* spoken of in our opening verse? John the Baptist stated that Jesus is *the Lamb of God who takes away the sin of the world!*[102] Sin He took away through His body *that was slain* for you and me. Ultimately, His willing, pure, sinless sacrifice for our sins deems Jesus worthy of power, riches, wisdom, might, honor, glory, and blessing.

Just as we have seen with God the Father, the Son is also due a genuine *fall-on-your-face* kind of adoration. We worship Jesus for everything He is within Himself and as our

---

[101] Revelation 5:11
[102] John 1:29

69

Powerful Creator, Blessed Savior, and Lord of All.

However, something remarkable strikes me in Revelation, Chapter 5. Jesus is the Lamb *that was slain*. One would imagine that being innocently murdered at the hands of your enemies would be a defeat. Yet, there He is, exalted upon the throne of God, and from Revelation 5:9, He is the only One worthy to take the scroll mentioned and break its seals.

Why is that? Jesus is worthy through having redeemed us with His blood. That He sits on the throne at the right hand of the Father is an example of God's economy. What was meant as the ultimate evil—the slaying of the Son of God—was the very thing that seated Him on His throne.

Jesus' rejection and abandonment by many, His betrayal, suffering, death, crucifixion, and burial in a dark tomb were meant for His destruction and, as far as the enemy of our soul was concerned, ours as well. However, God turned this horror against Him into good by raising Jesus bodily from the dead. What seemed a defeat to those who hated Him was for our redemption and His glory.

This brings us to another fascinating scene in Revelation 5. The Apostle John also witnessed:

Every created thing which is in heaven and on the earth and under the earth and on the sea, and all things in them, I heard saying, "To Him who sits on the throne, and to the Lamb, be blessing and honor and glory and dominion forever and ever."[103]

Notice the word *every*, which, when properly translated, means *every*. Not some, or a few, or only Jesus' believers confessed that blessing, honor, glory, and dominion are His forever and ever. Who will proclaim these things? Pharaoh, who told Moses, "*Who is the Lord that I should obey His voice to let Israel go?*"[104] will proclaim it. In the Book of Esther, Haman, who hated the Jewish people to the point of plotting to have them all wiped out, will proclaim that. All the prophets of Baal and Asherah, spoken of in 1 Kings 18, will proclaim the above. And even *the fool* who *has said in his heart*, "*There is no God*,"[105] will confess this.

You see, believer and unbeliever alike, living or even those who have died, will:

At the name of Jesus EVERY KNEE WILL BOW, of those who are in heaven and on earth and under the earth, and that every tongue will confess that Jesus Christ is Lord, to the glory of God the Father.[106]

---

[103] Revelation 5:13
[104] Exodus 5:2
[105] Psalms 14:1
[106] Philippians 2:10-11

Psalms 110:1 states, *The Lord says to my Lord: "Sit at My right hand until I make Your enemies a footstool for Your feet."* This statement referred to Jesus according to Hebrews 10:13 and elsewhere in the New Testament.

Simply because those who hated Jesus, and His people, will also proclaim that blessing, honor, glory, dominion are His forever and ever, does not mean they will say it as we do. They will only state this as a fact, as the Apostle James explained. *You believe that God is one. You do well; the demons also believe, and shudder.*[107] Incredible is it not that many *humans* do not even have the sense to shutter before Him.

Far better it will be for us who will exclaim these things to our Lord now with equal enthusiasm as those who fall with love before His throne. If you don't feel led to at this point, you will have no choice later on. Since *every* means *every*, that will include you too. How great it will be to proclaim Jesus worthy with the same zeal of the elders, rather than how it will be as prompted from the fear of the fallen.

And the four living creatures kept saying,
"Amen."
And the elders fell down and worshiped.
Revelation 5:14

---

[107] James 2:19

I saw underneath the altar the souls
of those who had been slain because
of the word of God, and because of the
testimony which they had maintained;
and they cried out with a loud voice, saying,
"How long, O Lord, holy and true,
will You refrain from judging and avenging
our blood on those who dwell on the earth?"
Revelation 6:9-10

DAY 19 ~ VENGEANCE IS HIS

There are many details throughout the Book of Revelation that pique our curiosity and imagination. Some have symbolic images, and some are literal in their meaning. The purpose of this book is not to grapple with those terms but to address what our eyewitness saw and reported, which can offer us lessons we can use today. Thus, we will consider the precious souls mentioned above in Revelation 6.

Our opening verse today expresses the cry of those martyred for their faith. Notice that these individuals *underneath the altar*, having a special place in Glory, were *slain* on two accounts. The first was *because of the word of God* that they preserved in their heart, and the second count was *because of the testimony which they had maintained*. These followers of

Christ actively gave and stood firm in their testimony to the point of martyrdom.

The persecution these souls suffered, and as witnesses of the suffering of their communities and loved ones, prompted them to ask how long will their persecutors and executioners continue unconstrained. To the pleas for justice on behalf of those who shed their blood for the One Whose blood was shed for them, we find the answer:

> There was given to each of them a white robe; and they were told that they should rest for a little while longer, until the number of their fellow servants and their brethren who were to be killed even as they had been, would be completed also.[108]

Knowing that we have a God of justice, they directed their petition to the only One with the answer. Judgment and justice are on their way, but rest and be patient. There are more of you to come.

In Revelation 14:7, as an angel declared, we find that our Lord is true to His Word.

> "Fear God, and give Him glory, because the hour of His judgment has come; worship Him who made the heaven and

---

[108] Revelation 6:11

the earth and sea and springs of waters."

The Lord's judgment is always in accordance with *His* timing.

> "'Vengeance is Mine, and retribution, in due time their foot will slip; for the day of their calamity is near, and the impending things are hastening upon them.' for the Lord will vindicate His people, and will have compassion on His servants, when He sees that their strength is gone, and there is none remaining, bond or free."[109]

The Apostle Peter, through the inspiration of the Holy Spirit, offers words that believer and unbeliever alike should take to heart:

> But by His word the present heavens and earth are being reserved for fire, kept for the day of judgment and destruction of ungodly men. But do not let this one fact escape your notice, beloved, that with the Lord one day is like a thousand years, and a thousand years like one day.
>
> The Lord is not slow about His promise, as some count slowness, but is patient toward you, not wishing for any to perish but for all to come to repentance.[110]

---

[109] Deuteronomy 32:35-36
[110] 2 Peter 3:7-9

The Lord will not only avenge the blood He shed through His suffering at the hands of wicked men but will also avenge those who shed their blood because of their faith and testimony of Him.

However, in the passage from Peter, we see the heart of God. He does not wish for *any to perish but for all to come to repentance.* Do we have this same heart? When we consider their eternal judgment and punishment, does it not prompt an urgency to see that many do not perish in their lost condition? Does it not give you the desire to see all come to repentance?

Unfortunately, our focus is so often on the things of this life that we forget what is to come. What we have looked at thus far in this resource should prepare our heart, soul, and mind for Christ's return, which is the purpose of this work. The goal is to set our mind on the things above, which will bring about radical revival in us and those with whom we share these great truths.

And they said to the mountains and to the rocks,
"Fall on us and hide us from the presence of
Him who sits on the throne, and from the wrath
of the Lamb; for the great day of their wrath has
come, and who is able to stand?"
Revelation 6:16-17

When the Lamb broke the seventh seal,
there was silence in heaven
for about half an hour.
Revelation 8:1

DAY 20 ~ THE COLLECTIVE GASP

pparently, heaven is a boisterous place where the volume is way up. As we learn from the book of Revelation, it is a place where we find *myriads of myriads, and thousands of thousands* of loud voices crying out with continual singing, praise, worship, and various proclamations to and of our great God. Some of the voices are so loud that one can compare them to *thunder* and *like the sound of many waters*. There are also musical instruments—trumpet blasts and harps. I praise God that our ears will be suited for the array of sounds and volume when we get there. I am sure we will not be able to help but spontaneously contribute to it all. Oh, what a glorious day that will be!

However, something that strikes me to my core is the image of our opening verse above. The timing is definite. As soon as the Lamb of God broke the last seal of judgment, there is silence in heaven for approximately one-half hour. I cannot imagine how peculiar it would be, in a place where the volume is not only up, but the voices and sounds are greatly multiplied, how it can suddenly become completely silent.

This scene, to me, is almost like a collective gasp. Nowhere in the Scriptures do we find that heaven ever fell silent, except in Revelation 8:1. We do not even read of this at the death or resurrection of our Lord. So unusual is this scene, John specifically documented it. Obviously, God the Holy Spirit specifically wanted this brief moment communicated to us since all Scripture is *God-breathed.*[111]

According to the book of Revelation, at the moment of their silence, one-quarter of Earth's population had already been destroyed. Yet, there was much more to come by way of terrible judgment. At this hush in heaven, a passage from Zechariah comes to mind. *"Be silent, all flesh, before the Lord; for He is aroused from His holy habitation."*[112]

There are times when it is very appropriate to keep silent. I am reminded of this exchange between the Lord God Almighty and a man named Job.

> The Lord said to Job, "Will the faultfinder contend with the Almighty? Let him who reproves God answer it."

---

[111] 2 Timothy 3:16 (AMP)
[112] Zechariah 2:13

Then Job answered the Lord and said, "Behold, I am insignificant; what can I reply to You? I lay my hand on my mouth. Once I have spoken, and I will not answer; Even twice, and I will add nothing more."[113]

Yet, I do not think that Job could ever have imagined the horrors on Earth that followed the silence John reported.

Jesus warned in Matthew 24:21-22:

"For then there will be a great tribulation, such as has not occurred since the beginning of the world until now, nor ever will. Unless those days had been cut short, no life would have been saved; but for the sake of the elect those days will be cut short."

The aftermath of the breaking of that seal is so shocking the mind can hardly comprehend it. The collective gasp and silence are understandable. The time for the Lamb's judgment was at hand. The silence, I believe, prompts soberness for us regarding the reality that those we know and love might suffer what John reported.

Unfortunately, we are keeping silent at the wrong time. Silence from us now is the last

---

[113] Job 40:1-5

thing this world needs. I think instead it is time to make the same request that the Apostle Paul did from a Roman prison:

Pray on my behalf, that utterance may be given to me in the opening of my mouth, to make known with boldness the mystery of the gospel, for which I am an ambassador in chains; that in proclaiming it I may speak boldly, as I ought to speak.[114]

If the Apostle Paul, while a prisoner of Rome, could request prayer for making a bold proclamation of the Gospel, ought we not effect the same petition for others and ourselves? Our silence has not helped us thus far. The more silent we become, the easier it is for those who oppose us to silence us further. No! Now is the time to *speak boldly* as we ought to and enjoy eternity with those we fervently pray will become one of the *myriads* of loud and passionate praise.

Then the angel took the censer and filled it with the fire of the altar, and threw it to the earth; and there followed peals of thunder and sounds and flashes of lightning and an earthquake. And the seven angels who had the seven trumpets prepared themselves to sound them.
Revelation 8:5-6

---

[114] Ephesians 6:18-19

*And the great dragon was thrown down,
the serpent of old who is called the devil and
Satan, who deceives the whole world;
he was thrown down to the earth,
and his angels were thrown down with him.*
Revelation 12:9

―――――⟲⟳―――――

DAY 21 ~ THE FATHER OF LIES

A t some point during the tribulation period, in the passage above, as the Apostle John reported, Satan, along with his angels, will be *thrown down to the earth*. Currently, the *serpent of old who is called the devil and Satan* is all about indictments against us before God as the Scriptures reveal.

One of the most significant examples of the deceiver at work was when Satan, after roaming the earth, then *presented himself before the Lord*, and set his sights on a righteous man named Job:

"But put forth Your hand now and touch all that he has; he will surely curse You to Your face."
Then the Lord said to Satan, "Behold, all that he has is in your power, only do

not put forth your hand on him."

So Satan departed from the presence of the Lord.[115]

Since Satan's first attempt at enticing Job to curse God failed miserably, Satan tried a second time:

Satan answered the Lord and said, "Skin for skin! Yes, all that a man has he will give for his life. However, put forth Your hand now, and touch his bone and his flesh; he will curse You to Your face."

So the Lord said to Satan, "Behold, he is in your power, only spare his life."[116]

The first thing we learn is that Satan does not give up. We can also understand this from the temptation of Christ in the wilderness as the Scriptures state, *When the devil had finished every temptation, he left Him **until an opportune time**.*[117] Satan is always looking for a more suitable time to trip us up. We also read about this in 1 Peter, along with some great advice.

Be of sober spirit, be on the alert. Your adversary, the devil, prowls around like a roaring lion, seeking someone to devour.

---

[115] Job 1:11-12
[116] Job 2:4-6
[117] Luke 4:13 (emphasis mine)

But resist him, firm in your faith, knowing that the same experiences of suffering are being accomplished by your brethren who are in the world.[118]

Wise advice from a man whom Jesus warned, *"Simon, Simon, behold, Satan has demanded permission to sift you like wheat."*[119] Now, if Satan demanded to *sift* Simon Peter, it only follows that he would attempt to make the same demand for us.

However, notice that Satan also had to seek *God's* permission. This is the second lesson we learn from Job and Jesus' caution to Peter. Satan's power to inflict is limited to God's authorization. He can do nothing against us without the Lord allowing him the ability.

Notice Satan does not give God permission, and neither do we. Satan is not co-equal with God. The devil does not have the exact attributes as God except that he is malevolent, where God is benevolent. No. Satan and the demons are in subjection to God. Jesus commanded demons into a herd of swine[120] and cast them out of the demoniacs of Matthew 17 and Luke 8.

Sometimes we lose sight of these truths and forget Satan only possesses one tool—the lie. Unfortunately, we happened to fall for it more

---

[118] 1 Peter 5:8-9
[119] Luke 22:31
[120] Matthew 8:31-32

often than not! Of Satan, Jesus alerted:

He was a murderer from the beginning, and does not stand in the truth because there is no truth in him. Whenever he speaks a lie, he speaks from his own nature, for he is a liar and the father of lies.[121]

Being the father of lies means that it originates from Satan and not God, which answers many who struggle with their faith. Did God create sin? The answer is, no, He did not. Sin originated with Satan, and as the father, or the source, of lies, the lie originated with him as well.

Though Satan can accuse the believer, we have the best Defense Attorney we could ever imagine! Jesus intercedes for us, which allows us to live victorious in Him. Though at one time dead in sin, we are now alive in Him!

Then I heard a loud voice in heaven, saying, "Now the salvation, and the power, and the kingdom of our God and the authority of His Christ have come, for the accuser of our brethren has been thrown down, he who accuses them before our God day and night."
Revelation 12:10

---

[121] John 8:44

"For this reason, rejoice,
O heavens and you who dwell in them.
Woe to the earth and the sea, because the devil
has come down to you, having great wrath,
knowing that he has only a short time."
Revelation 12:12

———— ❦ ————

DAY 22 ~ THE DEFEATED FOE

Satan's time is indeed short. I do not think it would be a significant risk to my credibility if I stated that he is well aware of this fact. The zeal with which he seems to be working in this, the twenty-first century, makes this easy to recognize.

One cannot witness the utter inhumanity and palpable hatred from specific sectors of our society and many others worldwide for the believer and miss the fact that Satan is hard at work turning people against each other. However, as we learned from Day 21, he does not act without God allowing him to, and thankfully, he is a defeated foe as 1 John 3:8 matter-of-factly explains:

The one who practices sin is of the devil; for the devil has sinned from the beginning. The Son of God appeared for this purpose, to destroy the works of the devil.

Sometimes, it is easy for us to forget that Satan was defeated at the death, burial, and resurrection of our Lord Jesus Christ. It seems to me many believers have a stronger fear of the devil than they do of God. I am always disheartened to hear professing believers, as they are praying to God the Father, will suddenly start rebuking Satan in the middle of their prayer to God! We, as believers, have nothing to say to this defeated foe, and certainly not during our conversation with God, as we find in Jude 9:

> But Michael the archangel, when he disputed with the devil and argued about the body of Moses, did not dare pronounce against him a railing judgment, but said, "The Lord rebuke you!"

The better tactic is to, *Submit therefore to God. Resist the devil and he will flee from you.*[122] Our Lord Jesus told us where our focus should be:

> "Do not rejoice in this, that the spirits are subject to you, but rejoice that your

---

[122] James 4:7

names are recorded in heaven."[123]

No matter how much satanic beings can oppress us, they cannot possess us. God will not share the temple of our body with the enemy of our soul, as we learn from 1 John 4:4.

> You are from God, little children, and have overcome them; because greater is He who is in you than he who is in the world.

And while our battle is against *the rulers, against the powers, against the world forces of this darkness, against the spiritual forces of wickedness in the heavenly places*[124] where we can feel that oppression or temptation, God provides us with tools, such as in Ephesians 6. Therefore, we can be confident that:

> No temptation has overtaken you but such as is common to man; and God is faithful, who will not allow you to be tempted beyond what you are able, but with the temptation will provide the way of escape also, so that you will be able to endure it.[125]

---

[123] Luke 10:20
[124] Ephesians 6:12
[125] 1 Corinthians 10:13 (Cultivate 2.0-E Group, did you commit this verse to memory?)

As we learn from Revelation 20:10, Satan will ultimately be cast into the *lake of fire* for all eternity. His judgment is coming. As many people incorrectly imagine, he is far from running the show! Satan is the chief prisoner. He is not forcing people in red jumpsuits to shovel coal. He is not the *tormentor*; rather, Satan will be the *tormented*!

Indeed, we have nothing to say to that defeated foe, the devil. Therefore, we stand before our God, leaning on Him and relying on the spiritual tools He provided. Additionally, we are encouraged by our Lord to rejoice that our *names are recorded in heaven* as we are about God's business of snatching from Satan's grasp those he would desire to sift like wheat.

And the devil who deceived them was thrown into the lake of fire and brimstone, where the beast and the false prophet are also; and they will be tormented day and night forever and ever.
Revelation 20:10

The rest of mankind, who were not killed by these plagues, did not repent of the works of their hands, so as not to worship demons, and the idols of gold and of silver and of brass and of stone and of wood, which can neither see nor hear nor walk; and they did not repent of their murders nor of their sorceries nor of their immorality nor of their thefts.
Revelation 9:20-21

DAY 23 ~ SHAKING THEIR FISTS

For many of us, as we read through the *Book of Revelation*, our hearts break for those who are suffering under such tremendous and horrifying judgments, ones the mind can hardly comprehend. However, keep in mind that the individuals in the above verses knew that God was in control. Yet they *did not repent*, a statement found four times in Revelation, showing they continued in defiance.

Should God withhold His hand of judgment on those who remain unrepentant and continue in willful sin? What of these sins? In short, the unrepentant engaged in demon worship, idolatry, sorceries, immorality, theft, and even murder. In looking at the first three from this list, we cannot escape God's view:

> "There shall not be found among you anyone who makes his son or his daughter pass through the fire, one who uses divination, one who practices witchcraft, or one who interprets omens, or a sorcerer, or one who casts a spell, or a medium, or a spiritist, or one who calls up the dead. For whoever does these things is detestable to the Lord."[126]

Those who rely upon the occult, choosing Satan as their father rather than God, will have overwhelming demonic activity unleashed upon them. Those individuals who call upon demonic spirits, looking to them for guidance, and who worship them will ultimately experience torments to their destruction.

Demons do not have the power to use God for their purposes. God will use these entities, which unrepentant people pursue, for His divine judgment. Ultimately, however, Satan's minions will be condemned just as he will. The havoc demons wreak will come to a sure end.

Regarding the sexual immorality of the unrepentant, one need only look at the destruction of Sodom and Gomorrah and a

---

[126] Deuteronomy 18:10-12

review of Romans, Chapter 1, which reveals a slippery slope to depravity.

Unrepentant sexually immoral persons, according to Romans 1, give hearty approval for others to join them in an attempt to make their iniquity the norm. However, we learn from Paul to *flee immorality*. Why is that? Because *every other sin that a man commits is outside the body, but the immoral man sins against his own body.*[127]

We cannot help but also notice, among that terrible list of sins above, included is that of theft. Apparently, this is how they accumulated their vast wealth. They stole it from others in the same manner, I imagine as the property, wealth, expensive artwork, and lives that the Jewish people were victims of during the Holocaust. This is what evil people will do. They steal the wealth of others to line their own pockets.

As murder is among the list above, and as was already covered, the judgments we see during the tribulation period will avenge the blood the martyrs shed.

And I heard the angel of the waters saying, "Righteous are You, who are and who were, O Holy One, because You

---

[127] 1 Corinthians 6:18

judged these things; for they poured out the blood of saints and prophets, and You have given them blood to drink. They deserve it."[128]

Did you catch that? *They deserve it.* These people are entirely unrepentant. They are hardened to the point of shaking their fists at God continually even though they know He is the One in control and can stop it.

If the torment that will befall the people on earth during the time of the tribulation is disturbing to you, perhaps it is time to share Christ with them without counting the cost. They are pawns of our adversary, the devil.

Where is our heart for the lost? We can no longer sit idly by while we know individuals who might well suffer the horrors of judgment are in our family and neighborhood. It is time to realize that living in the last days is our reality and therefore we must purposefully reach as many as we can for Christ today.

"But for the cowardly and unbelieving and abominable and murderers and immoral persons and sorcerers and idolaters and all liars, their part will be in the lake that burns with fire and brimstone, which is the second death."
Revelation 21:8

---

[128] Revelation 16:5-6

He performs great signs, so that he even makes
fire come down out of heaven to the earth in
the presence of men. And he deceives those who
dwell on the earth because of the signs which it
was given him to perform in the presence of the
beast, telling those who dwell on the earth to
make an image to the beast who had the
wound of the sword and has come to life.
Revelation 13:13-14

DAY 24 ~ TICKLISH EYES AND EARS

As we read the passage above, we realize how important it is to be in God's Word and have the Word of God in us. We do not have to be an expert on the cults or the occult to spot what is contrary to God's Word. Those who are in the Word and are filled with the Holy Spirit can immediately spot spiritual deception and false doctrine.

Unfortunately, many people are biblically ignorant, believing they do not have the time or the need to open a Bible. Sadly, this is also the state of the Church in America.

However, believers who do take His Word to heart, and try to be good students of it, realize we were forewarned to the deception we read in the opening passage for today:

> The one whose coming is in accord with the activity of Satan, with all power and signs and false wonders, and with all the deception of wickedness for those who perish, because they did not receive the love of the truth so as to be saved.
>
> For this reason God will send upon them a deluding influence so that they will believe what is false, in order that they all may be judged who did not believe the truth, but took pleasure in wickedness.[129]

At this point, one might well ask, *Will deception be confined to the tribulation period? If not, could the deception entice current believers?* Again, the importance of knowing the Scriptures in these, the last days, is vital. The Apostle Paul spelled it out to a young man named Timothy:

> The time will come when they will not endure sound doctrine; but wanting to have their ears tickled, they will accumulate for themselves teachers in

---

[129] 2 Thessalonians 2:9-12

accordance to their own desires, and will turn away their ears from the truth and will turn aside to myths.[130]

It is much easier to sit in the pews of a fellowship and have someone do all the thinking for us, especially if they have a charismatic personality and a following of thousands worldwide. Such was the case with a man named Jose Luis de Jesus Miranda.

Born in Ponce, Puerto Rico in 1947, Miranda moved to Miami in 1986, becoming the headliner for his *Growing in Grace* cult. In 2004, he stated that not only was he Jesus Christ, but he was also the "ultimate authority on the Gospel."

By 2007, Miranda tattooed his arm with the number *666*, with over two dozen of his followers doing likewise, as he then declared himself the Antichrist. By 2013, he was dead, proving that Miranda was neither the Christ nor the Antichrist, although indeed *an* antichrist, he was also another blind guide and deceiver.

While the deception of Jose Luis de Jesus Miranda is evident for many reading this book, thousands of individuals globally still fell for it. However, some deceivers who are alive today, or who are on their way, are a little more subtle. The following is a sober warning from

---

[130] 2 Timothy 4:3-4

our Lord Jesus Christ:

"False Christs and false prophets will arise and will show great signs and wonders, so as to mislead, if possible, even the elect. Behold, I have told you in advance."[131]

While it is not possible to deceive the elect, it sure is possible for those around us to be deceived. Pews are plentiful with folks who would rather have their ears tickled than to study the truth. Since we know that *Satan disguises himself as an angel of light*[132] even to the point of working signs and miracles, our job is to *examine everything carefully; hold fast to that which is good.*[133]

Beloved, do not believe every spirit, but test the spirits to see whether they are from God, because many false prophets have gone out into the world. By this you know the Spirit of God: every spirit that confesses that Jesus Christ has come in the flesh is from God; and every spirit that does not confess Jesus is not from God; this is the spirit of the antichrist, of which you have heard that it is coming, and now it is already in the world.

1 John 4:1-3

---

[131] Matthew 24:24-25
[132] 2 Corinthians 11:14
[133] Thessalonians 5:21

*I took the little book out of the angel's hand and
ate it, and in my mouth it was sweet as honey;
and when I had eaten it, my stomach
was made bitter. And they said to me,
"You must prophesy again concerning many
peoples and nations and tongues and kings."*
Revelation 10:10-11

DAY 25 ~ BITTERSWEET

Our opening passage for today is one that struck me. This passage in the book of Revelation is similar to a scene in the commissioning of Ezekiel. While it is sweet to speak on behalf of the Lord, the message itself had to be a bitter pill, or rather scroll, to swallow:

> "Now you, son of man, listen to what I am speaking to you; do not be rebellious like that rebellious house. Open your mouth and eat what I am giving you."
>
> When He spread it out before me, it was written on the front and back, and written on it were lamentations, mourning and woe.[134]
>
> "Son of man, feed your stomach and fill your body with this scroll which I am

---

[134] Ezekiel 2:8,10

giving you." Then I ate it, and it was sweet as honey in my mouth.[135]

From swallowing the sweet book that made his belly bitter, the Apostle John knew the weight of the message he was to prophesy just as Ezekiel did. Digesting that little book would prepare John for the bittersweet message he was commissioned to deliver to the world.

Like communion, ingesting something makes it more meaningful and causes us to pause and consider the seriousness of it all. By consuming it, it becomes part of us. For John, how sweet it was knowing that the time of judgment for evil was at hand, but how bitter to his soul would be the images and horrors that an unrepentant world would face.

Jesus commissioned all who believed and received Him to, *"Go into all the world and preach the gospel to all creation."*[136] While the gospel is sweet for salvation, it is bitter to our hearts for those who refuse to repent because we know the reality of where they will spend their eternity.

For many of our martyred brothers and sisters around the globe, the testimony on their lips and the life they gave was sweet and precious, but what they suffered as the

---

135 Ezekiel 3:3
136 Mark 16:15

persecuted church lies bitter in our stomach.

When we look at the United States border, as we have people flooding into our country, perhaps missionaries with the desire to reach others for Christ will not have to go too far after all. Right at our border is an enormous opportunity for ministry. Do you imagine the Lord is unaware of this? Our fellow citizens who can speak the language of those coming across can make a significant impact for Christ.

When we live in a rural community that is suddenly growing with a multitude of families moving in, do we lament because it is not as peaceful as it used to be? Or, do we recognize the opportunity to share the gospel with our new neighbors?

As we witness the cults going door to door, sharing a lie, do we as believers hide behind the couch when our doorbell rings? When one of those cults has set over a dozen dates as to when *Armageddon* will happen, that tells me this is a group wholly consumed with the last days, which means they are ripe for harvest. We, who have the Truth, should not be hiding behind our couch!

John's responsibility to prophesy, or to tell the world, is our responsibility as well. We are accountable for the knowledge we have;

therefore, we cannot remain silent. God has given each one of us a powerful testimony. Every believer has a unique way in which God has brought us to Himself.

Now is not a time for us to avoid reading or speaking about the reality of the last days because we imagine no one will believe or understand it. Now is the time for us to reach out with urgency and recognize the opportunities God is bringing right to our very doorstep. Even though the message of sin and death is bitter to those who first hear it, how sweet it is to offer them salvation via our Great God and our Savior, the Lord Jesus Christ.

"All authority has been given to Me in heaven and on earth. Go therefore and make disciples of all the nations, baptizing them in the name of the Father and the Son and the Holy Spirit, teaching them to observe all that I commanded you; and lo, I am with you always, even to the end of the age."
Matthew 28:18-20

> *"The kingdom of the world has become the kingdom of our Lord and of His Christ; and He will reign forever and ever."*
> Revelation 11:15

DAY 26 ~ ETERNAL SHOULDERS

Forever and ever. The concept of the eternal has always been difficult for our finite minds to grasp. A God Who was, is, and will be forever and ever, is a challenge to comprehend for beings whose existence often revolves around a clock.

However, anyone familiar with George Frideric Handel's *The Hallelujah Chorus* cannot help but sing the opening verse as they read it, understanding that the victory over the kingdoms and governments of our present world will *become the kingdom of our Lord and of His Christ.* This will be the case not for a decade, or a few centuries, or even for a millennium, but *He will reign forever and ever.*

As we search the Scriptures, allowing them to interpret themselves, we find another passage that George Frideric Handel put to music in his oratorio, *Messiah.* However, I included for context the verse he left out:

For a child will be born to us, a son will be given to us; and the government will rest on His shoulders; and His name will be called Wonderful Counselor, Mighty God, Eternal Father, Prince of Peace.

There will be no end to the increase of His government or of peace, on the throne of David and over his kingdom, to establish it and to uphold it with justice and righteousness from then on and forevermore. The zeal of the Lord of hosts will accomplish this.[137]

Christ's Kingdom will be *forevermore*. This Messianic prophecy, advising us that He is Mighty God and the Eternal Father (or preeminent over eternity), informs us that *the government* will be on *His* shoulders and *His* shoulders, alone.

"Then I will set the key of the house of David on his shoulder, when he opens no one will shut, when he shuts no one will open. I will drive him like a peg in a firm place, and he will become a throne of glory to his father's house."[138]

---

[137] Isaiah 9:6-7
[138] Isaiah 22:22-23

Does that sound familiar? As outlined in Day 12, when we addressed Jesus' *key*, I used this passage and recognize that it is useful when focusing on another aspect of our Lord. The weight of the government upon His shoulders will not be too much for Him to handle. His shoulders are big enough, and worthy enough, to carry the government Himself, forever and ever. Since He alone is worthy and has the *key*, Jesus will not need anyone else to help Him bear it.

Though the Scriptures state that we will reign with Christ,[139] however, the government is not on *our* shoulders as well. Isaiah 9:6-7 is a focus on the Messiah, Who gives His glory to no other.[140] As a governor's relationship is with the president, there remains subordination. They are not equal in authority, responsibility, or honor due.

Our challenge is that our focus is often more on the temporal; therefore, we can miss the weight of the eternal as a reality. We look at the governments of this world and curse the darkness, forgetting what will come *forever and ever.*

As we have learned, Satan is not only all

---

[139] Revelation 20:6, 22:5
[140] Isaiah 42:8

about the lie; he is about obsessing us with the future. This is a primary focus for the occult with its Ouija boards, Tarot cards, and fortunetellers.

If your focus is on this life and its troubles alone, you will forget the forever and ever that awaits us. The government is on His shoulders. Have peace. He will reign forever and ever. Get excited. The Scriptures state that we will reign with Him. That is amazing! Perhaps we need the attitude of the elders and fall on our face before Him and realize, Jesus has got this, including you and me, for all eternity!

And the twenty-four elders,
who sit on their thrones before God,
fell on their faces and worshiped God, saying,
"We give You thanks, O Lord God,
the Almighty, who are and who were,
because You have taken Your great power
and have begun to reign."
Revelation 11:16-17

*And the dragon stood before the woman who
was about to give birth, so that when she gave
birth he might devour her child.
And she gave birth to a son, a male child, who is
to rule all the nations with a rod of iron;
and her child was caught up to God and to His
throne. Then the woman fled into the wilderness
where she had a place prepared by God, so that
there she would be nourished for one thousand
two hundred and sixty days.*
Revelation 12:4-6

DAY 27 ~ WINGS OF PROTECTION

The enmity between Satan and our Lord
Jesus Christ and his people, Israel, goes
back to the Garden of Eden. Yet God's
protection and provision for all those who love
Him always prevails.

Before God had formed Eve, He
commanded Adam not to eat the fruit from the
Tree of the Knowledge of Good and Evil. After
Eve was fashioned from Adam's rib, the serpent
in the grass slithered upon the scene and
beguiled Adam's newly formed bride. As she
ate the fruit, Adam did not protect her or
remind her of God's command. Therefore, *she*

gave also to her husband with her, and he ate.[141]
Thus, in Genesis 3, we read of the tragic fall of humankind. The husband, wife, animals, all of creation would fall under the shadow of the curse. Nevertheless, God's final words to the serpent offered hope:

> "Because you have done this, cursed are you more than all cattle, and more than every beast of the field; On your belly you will go, and dust you will eat All the days of your life; And I will put enmity between you and the woman, and between your seed and her seed; He shall bruise you on the head, And you shall bruise him on the heel."[142]

This, the first Messianic prophecy, was fulfilled with the bruising of Christ's heel upon the cross, the only execution method that does bruise the heel. This is also where Jesus dealt a crushing blow to Satan's head whereby redeeming humanity from the clutches of sin and death by His glorious resurrection. Indeed, because of Jesus' sacrifice for us, we may cry, *"DEATH IS SWALLOWED UP in victory. O DEATH, WHERE IS YOUR VICTORY? O DEATH, WHERE IS YOUR STING?"*[143]

The Messiah's sacrificial death for His people

---

[141] Genesis 3:6
[142] Genesis 3:14-15
[143] 1 Corinthians 15:54-55

and the world would not have happened if God had not protected Jesus from Herod. After the magi had visited the Christ Child, God warned them in a dream not to return to Herod. Therefore, *they left for their own country by another way.*[144]

God also sent an angel of the Lord to Joseph in a dream, instructing him to take Mary and the Child and escape from Herod's rage to Egypt. God intervened, and the Child survived.

In Daniel 10:21, we read that Michael, Israel's national guardian angel, stands against hostile spiritual forces to protect and defend.[145] In an epic battle in Revelation 12, we read that Michael and his angels prevailed over Satan and his minions, and they were cast out of heaven.

We have seen God's rescue and provision for Israel throughout the Scriptures. We then read these precious words from God, Himself:

"Thus you shall say to the house of Jacob and tell the sons of Israel: 'You yourselves have seen what I did to the Egyptians, and how I bore you on eagles' wings, and brought you to Myself.'"[146]

"For the Lord's portion is His people; Jacob is the allotment of His inheritance. He found him in a desert land, and in the howling waste of a wilderness; He

---

[144] Matthew 2:12
[145] Daniel 10:21 (AMP)
[146] Exodus 19:3-4

encircled him, He cared for him, He guarded him as the pupil of His eye. Like an eagle that stirs up its nest, that hovers over its young, He spread His wings and caught them, He carried them on His pinions. The Lord alone guided him, and there was no foreign god with him."[147]

However, is there a recent example of God intervening and protecting His people? I believe so. In December 2016, videos emerged of a thick, dark, storm cloud of dust and rain that fell upon the border of Syria but did not enter Israel's Golan Heights, where the terrorist group, ISIS, had previously attacked. This barrier stopped ISIS from a planned invasion.[148] Interesting, isn't it?

We no longer fear death or Satan. His minions have no power over us. God is in complete control, and I am reminded of Psalms 125:2, *As the mountains surround Jerusalem, So the Lord surrounds His people from this time forth and forever.* And ever, Amen!

But the two wings of the great eagle were given to the woman, so that she could fly into the wilderness to her place, where she was nourished for a time and times and half a time, from the presence of the serpent.
Revelation 12:1

---

[147] Deuteronomy 32:9-12
[148] https://www.youtube.com/watch?v=Y5I-QKuF9OM

"Behold, I am coming quickly,
and My reward is with Me, to render to
every man according to what he has done"
Revelation 22:12

DAY 28 ~ ETERNAL REWARDS

When considering the Holy City, the New Jerusalem, it is overwhelming to realize that our Lord will also add to us rewards for service. Especially because, according to Revelation 21:7, that glorious city is also a part of our inheritance.

John described the Holy City as *brilliance like a very costly stone, as a stone of crystal-clear jasper.*[149] For *fifteen hundred miles; its length and width and height are equal.*[150] *The material of the wall—jasper; and the city pure gold, like clear glass. The foundation stones of the city wall—adorned with every kind of precious stone.*[151] *And the twelve gates—twelve pearls. And the street of the city—pure gold, like transparent glass.*[152]

There is *no temple in it, for the Lord God the Almighty and the Lamb are its temple. And the city has no need of the sun or of the moon to*

---

[149] Revelation 21:11
[150] Revelation 21:16
[151] Revelation 21:18-19
[152] Revelation 21:21

shine on it, for the glory of God has illumined it, and its lamp is the Lamb.[153] Incredibly, there is more to add to what our eyewitness, the Apostle John, described!

Jesus promised, *"In My Father's house are many dwelling places; if it were not so, I would have told you; for I go to prepare a place for you. If I go and prepare a place for you, I will come again and receive you to Myself, that where I am, there you may be also."*[154]

As if a home of our own, built by God, Himself, were not enough, our great God and Savior, Jesus Christ, has promised us personal rewards as well, as we read in our opening text for today. Jesus said in Mark 10:29-3:

> "Truly I say to you, there is no one who has left house or brothers or sisters or mother or father or children or farms, for My sake and for the gospel's sake, but that he will receive a hundred times as much now in the present age, houses and brothers and sisters and mothers and children and farms, along with persecutions; and in the age to come, eternal life. But many who are first will be last, and the last, first."

Once again, we are faced with God's economy as being very different from our own.

---

[153] Revelation 21:22-23
[154] John 14:2-3

In our economy, those who have the large, visible, international ministries will be at the head of the line. Then somehow, we believe that the gal who quietly serves her family, and is faithful to bring cookies and punch to the next potluck, will be way in the back.

However, according to Jesus, *"For whoever gives you a cup of water to drink because of your name as followers of Christ, truly I say to you, he will not lose his reward."*[155] How much more so for punch?

The point is, *your Father who sees what is done in secret will reward you.*[156] He who knows our thoughts and the intents also knows the motivation for why we serve as no church elder could. *Now he who plants and he who waters are one; but each will receive his own reward according to his own labor.*[157]

Not only will we inherit the Holy City with our Great God as the glory of it all for eternity, but according to Revelation 22:14, we will also have the right to eat of the *Tree of Life*. The tree from which Adam and Eve were barred, we will partake. We, who are cleansed in the blood Christ shed for us, will have the right to stroll through the gates of the Holy City. Incredible to comprehend—promised by God.

With all we have to look forward to in view, what should our response be? How does this

---

[155] Mark 9:41
[156] Matthew 6:4
[157] 1 Corinthians 3:8

affect us today? How can we prepare for so great a reward and inheritance? I believe we find the answers in Colossians, Corinthians, and Hebrews, reminding us how important it is to be in the Word as we fully prepare for Christ's return.

Whatever you do, do your work heartily, as for the Lord rather than for men, knowing that from the Lord you will receive the reward of the inheritance. It is the Lord Christ whom you serve.[158]

Therefore, my beloved brethren, be steadfast, immovable, always abounding in the work of the Lord, knowing that your toil is not in vain in the Lord.[159]

For God is not unjust so as to forget your work and the love which you have shown toward His name, in having ministered and in still ministering to the saints.[160]

"Blessed are you when men hate you, and ostracize you, and insult you, and scorn your name as evil, for the sake of the Son of Man.
Be glad in that day and leap for joy,
for behold, your reward is great in heaven."
Luke 6:22-23

---

[158] Colossians 3:23-24
[159] 1 Corinthians 15:58
[160] Hebrews 6:10

*"And behold, I am coming quickly.
Blessed is he who heeds the words
of the prophecy of this book."*
Revelation 22:7

DAY 29 ~ READ AND HEED

Five times in the book of Revelation, Jesus stated that He is coming quickly, meaning one of two things. Either it would not be long before He gets here from the time of His ascension into heaven, or He will return quickly once events concerning Revelation begin to unfold.

In Revelation 1:1, the Apostle John stated that he was recording what God gave *him to show to His bond-servants, the things which must soon take place.* He then wrote in Revelation 1:3, *for the time is near.*

Jesus then told John to *"Write the things which you have seen, and the things which are, and the things which will take place after these things."[161]*

When considering the above passages, one thing is clear, when Jesus does return, it should be of no surprise, and immediately my mind turns to Jesus' parable of the ten virgins, a parable that haunted me as an unbeliever:

---

[161] Revelation 1:19

"The kingdom of heaven will be comparable to ten virgins, who took their lamps and went out to meet the bridegroom. Five of them were foolish, and five were prudent. For when the foolish took their lamps, they took no oil with them, but the prudent took oil in flasks along with their lamps.

"Now while the bridegroom was delaying, they all got drowsy and began to sleep. But at midnight there was a shout, 'Behold, the bridegroom! Come out to meet him.'

"Then all those virgins rose and trimmed their lamps. The foolish said to the prudent, 'Give us some of your oil, for our lamps are going out.'

"But the prudent answered, 'No, there will not be enough for us and you too; go instead to the dealers and buy some for yourselves.'

"And while they were going away to make the purchase, the bridegroom came, and those who were ready went in with him to the wedding feast; and the door was shut. Later the other virgins also came, saying, 'Lord, lord, open up for us.'

"But he answered, 'Truly I say to you, I do not know you.'

Be on the alert then, for you do not

know the day nor the hour."[162]

I could not fathom the horror of not being prepared at that moment. To be standing there, lamp in hand, before a locked door. Why did this happen to them? Because they did not think this night would be *the* night, therefore they did not believe any preparation was necessary.

Interestingly, we can easily set aside a book in the Bible that we think might be too confusing and mystifying to digest or too frightening to consider. Perhaps we believe it is irrelevant to our lives today.

In our opening passage, Jesus said that the one *who heeds the words of the prophesy of this book* would be blessed. What book is that? It is *The Revelation of Jesus Christ*. However, if you do not read it, you cannot *heed* it.

Why would any believer choose to set aside a book containing information communicated by Jesus concerning His return, explicitly written to the churches? This seems like insider information to the extreme!

The Revelation of Jesus Christ is not a difficult book of the Bible to read. What is an allegory is an allegory. What is a simile is a simile. What is literal, we are to interpret literally. While we can debate certain aspects, whenever we begin to adjust the Scriptures to mean something that

---

[162] Matthew 25:1-13

it does not or to suit our means, we will find ourselves in dangerous territory.

I testify to everyone who hears the words of the prophecy of this book: if any one adds to them, God will add to him the plagues which are written in this book; and if anyone takes away from the words of the book of this prophecy, God will take away his part from the tree of life and from the holy city, which are written in this book.[163]

That is about as serious as it gets. The book of Revelation is necessary for the believer since it outlines what will *shortly take place* no matter how *quickly* it does or does not happen. Therefore we need to be in it and take it to heart. Reading and studying Revelation will prepare our hearts to meet Jesus, not just on that day, but every day until He comes.

*"These words are faithful and true";
and the Lord, the God of the spirits of
the prophets, sent His angel to show
to His bond-servants the things
which must soon take place.*
Revelation 22:6

---

[163] Revelation 22:18-19

*"Behold, the tabernacle of God is among men, and
He will dwell among them, and they
shall be His people, and God Himself will
be among them, and He will wipe away every
tear from their eyes; and there will no longer
be any death; there will no longer
be any mourning, or crying, or pain;
the first things have passed away."*
Revelation 21:3-4

DAY 30 ~ ALL THINGS NEW

Revelation 21:3-4, our opening passage, is the beautiful culmination of everything we long for and is promised by God. The omnipotent, omniscient, omnipresent God Almighty desires to dwell or *tabernacle* among us. The reason for all we read throughout the Scriptures, the ultimate purpose for creation, and especially us, is that God, Himself, desires to *tabernacle* with those He made in His image and who will respond to His offer of salvation. If you have ever had challenges with self-worth, I would think that a full embracing of this fact would dispel it quite nicely.

To confirm fully that we would understand God's intentions toward us and that the Apostle

John would get it right, *a loud voice from the throne*[164] that communicated our opening passage for today stated something important in three different ways.

> *God is among men.*
> *He will dwell among them.*
> *God Himself will be among them.*

That alone is worth pausing right now to offer a hearty, *Hallelujah!* God's desire is an intimate relationship with you and me. For some of us, we have family members who do not choose to be around us. We have neighbors who would rather avoid our company. We even have folks in our fellowship who would rather sit somewhere else. However, despite all God knows so intimately about His fallen, broken creatures:

> "God so loved the world, that He gave His only begotten Son, that whoever believes in Him shall not perish, but have eternal life. For God did not send the Son into the world to judge the world, but that the world might be saved through Him."[165]

God the Father gave His one and only Son

---

an extreme price to pay to *tabernacle* among us. But wait—there's more.

In Revelation 21:4, God *will wipe away every tear from* our *eyes*; tears He holds precious. Just as He has every hair on our head numbered,[166] Psalms 56:8 is a beautiful picture of God's accounting of every tear we shed. *You have taken account of my wanderings; put my tears in Your bottle. Are they not in Your book?* As He wipes away every tear from our eyes, God will also wipe away every memory of what caused them as well.

> "For behold, I create new heavens and a new earth; and the former things will not be remembered or come to mind. But be glad and rejoice forever in what I create; for behold, I create Jerusalem for rejoicing and her people for gladness. I will also rejoice in Jerusalem and be glad in My people; and there will no longer be heard in her the voice of weeping and the sound of crying."[167]

We are not going to remember the sorrows of loss through our sin, or physical and emotional pain we've endured, or the death of those we love, or even our death. In addition, as God will wipe our memory clean of these

---

[166] Luke 12:7
[167] Isaiah 65:17-19

things, God stated, *"FOR I WILL BE MERCIFUL TO THEIR INIQUITIES, AND I WILL REMEMBER THEIR SINS NO MORE."*[168]

It is no wonder many people believe that they would be bored in heaven. Could it be that they waste much of their lives worrying about, and crying over, the things of this life?

Terrible physical pain plagues many of us, to the extent that we cannot imagine our lives without it, yet as we tabernacle with Him, pain will not be a memory. Then there is emotional heartbreak over wayward children, emotional trauma over the loss of a child, parent, or spouse. We shed many tears throughout our lifetime. However, God will wipe them all away, the cause of them in our mind, and make all things new—including our present, ailing bodies as we will receive new ones suitable for eternity. What a great cause to rejoice!

Behold, I tell you a mystery; we will not all sleep,
but we will all be changed, in a moment, in the
twinkling of an eye, at the last trumpet;
for the trumpet will sound, and the dead will be
raised imperishable, and we will be changed.
For this perishable must put on the imperishable,
and this mortal must put on immortality.
1 Corinthians 15:51-53

---

[168] Hebrews 8:12

The Spirit and the bride say, "Come."
And let the one who hears say, "Come."
And let the one who is thirsty come;
let the one who wishes take the
water of life without cost.
Revelation 22:17

———— ❧ ————

DAY 31 ~ TO THE OVERCOMER

Humanitys' greatest desire has always been, and will always be, whether anyone wishes to admit it or not, a relationship with the living God. Unfortunately, after humanity's fall in the garden, we tend to run the other way, all the while having what Blaise Pascal referred to as *a god-shaped vacuum*. Humankind makes extraordinary attempts to fill that terrible void with anything else but God until we finally realize that He truly is the only One Who can.

As the various animals were brought to Adam, and he would find no suitable correspondence for companionship, we go through the same thing, as we draw to ourselves what is so beneath us, and God, as we find in Romans 1.

For even though they knew God, they did not honor Him as God or give thanks, but they became futile in their speculations, and their foolish heart was darkened. Professing to be wise, they became fools, and exchanged the glory of the incorruptible God for an image in the form of corruptible man and of birds and four-footed animals and crawling creatures.[169]

That which is below us, which we were to *rule over*, is not an equal exchange for an enormously elevated relationship with our Creator. The good news is that God does not give up on us that easily.

"I permitted Myself to be sought by those who did not ask for Me; I permitted Myself to be found by those who did not seek Me. I said, 'Here am I, here am I,' To a nation which did not call on My name. I have spread out My hands all day long to a rebellious people, who walk in the way which is not good, following their own thoughts, a people who continually provoke Me to My face."[170]

---

[169] Romans 1:21-23
[170] Isaiah 65:1-3

Does that sound familiar? Does it not suit us today? We are in a, *choose you this day whom you will serve*, moment. Therefore, we should:

> Seek the Lord while He may be found; call upon Him while He is near. Let the wicked forsake his way and the unrighteous man his thoughts; and let him return to the Lord, and He will have compassion on him, and to our God, for He will abundantly pardon. [171]

We need to be a bride ready with plenty of oil in our lamp and our gown made white— cleansed in Jesus' precious blood as we eagerly cry, "*Come, Lord Jesus, come!*" Sadly, some things get in the way of that preparation, namely, our sin.

The best way to prepare for Christ's return is through genuine repentance. That is His message to five of the seven churches in the book of Revelation. Once we repent, we then persevere, and with repentance and perseverance, we then join the camp of those who overcome. In the event of any difficulty remembering what Jesus, Himself, promised to overcomers, the lengthy list is as follows:

---

[171] Isaiah 55:6-7

"To him who overcomes, I will grant to eat of the tree of life which is in the Paradise of God."[172]

"He who overcomes will not be hurt by the second death."[173]

"To him who overcomes, to him I will give some of the hidden manna, and I will give him a white stone, and a new name written on the stone which no one knows but he who receives it."[174]

"He who overcomes, and he who keeps My deeds until the end, TO HIM I WILL GIVE AUTHORITY OVER THE NATIONS; AND HE SHALL RULE THEM WITH A ROD OF IRON, AS THE VESSELS OF THE POTTER ARE BROKEN TO PIECES, as I also have received authority from My Father; and I will give him the morning star."[175]

"He who overcomes will thus be clothed in white garments; and I will not erase his name from the book of life, and I will confess his name before My Father and before His angels."[176]

"He who overcomes, I will make him a pillar in the temple of My God, and he will not go out from it anymore; and I will

---

[172] Revelation 2:7
[173] Revelation 2:11
[174] Revelation 2:17
[175] Revelation 2:26-28
[176] Revelation 3:5

write on him the name of My God, and the name of the city of My God."[177]

"He who overcomes, I will grant to him to sit down with Me on My throne, as I also overcame and sat down with My Father on His throne."[178]

"He who overcomes will inherit these things, and I will be his God and he will be My son."[179]

Spelled out in order, one promise after another, it is pretty overwhelming. Perhaps a time for self-reflection is in order. With our Lord's promises in mind, we must ask ourselves, *Is my sin worth losing all that?*

When we repent of our sins and genuinely give our lives to Christ, it is so much easier for us to communicate that heartfelt cry of our opening verse to our Lord, *"Come!"*

Since we know the Lord is coming, and for Him, it will be shortly concerning time, what should our response be?

"Do not seal up the words of the prophecy of this book, for the time is near."[180] If the Apostle John was not to seal up the words written in the book of Revelation, then we should read

---

[177] Revelation 3:12
[178] Revelation 3:21
[179] Revelation 21:7
[180] Revelation 22:10

and unseal it from our lips, as well. It has been unsealed for us! Our Lord made it very personal. *"I, Jesus, have sent My angel to testify to you these things for the churches."*[181] How can we neglect so great a gift, so great a book, and so great a Lord?

Christ's declaration should prompt from us the same passionate cry as in our opening verse for the last day of this book and these, the last days before eternity. May we cry to those who do not know Him, *Come!* — come to the Lord Jesus Christ. Come to receive eternal life. Come with all who love Him and be with Him and us in that Holy City.

The Holy Spirit is giving that invitation, and we, as believers, must extend that invitation while there is still time. The great news is that invitation comes without cost because Christ already paid it in full. The invitation we extend is not simply to our next potluck, but it is to a vibrant relationship with our Lord Jesus Christ for the forgiveness of sins and eternal life with Him. This is how Revelation is relevant for our lives—today and on into eternity.

He who testifies to these things says,
"Yes, I am coming quickly."
Amen. Come, Lord Jesus.
The grace of the Lord Jesus be with all. Amen.
Revelation 22:20-21

---

[181] Revelation 22:16

ABOUT THE AUTHOR

Judy Salisbury, Founder and President of Logos Presentations, has been equipping Christians to share the gospel more effectively while helping believers live a vibrant life in the faith since the start of her multifaceted organization in 1994. This former radio talk show host has served on her local fire department since 2005 and volunteers in various roles, including a firefighter, EMT, and Crisis Care Counselor.

Judy speaks nationally on various topics such as Christian living, apologetics, and emotional trauma for secular and faith-based audiences. She is the author of several works, including *Calamity Care*, *More Than Devotion*, *Reasons for Faith*, *Engaging Encounters*, and *The Emmaus Conversation*.

Judy and her husband, Jeff, are proud parents and grandparents who enjoy family marshmallow roasts as they look forward to Christ's return at their home on the outskirts of the majestic Mount Saint Helens Volcanic National Park in Washington State.

For more information or to schedule
Judy Salisbury for your event, please visit:
www.LogosPresentations.com

Reasons For Faith

Answering Objections
And Obstacles to Belief

JUDY
SALISBURY

FOREWORD BY
DR NORMAN GEISLER

Engaging Encounters

Your Guide to Apply Reasons for Faith

Judy Salisbury

FOREWORD BY DR. DAVID GEISLER

THE EMMAUS CONVERSATION

AN EYEWITNESS ACCOUNT

FROM THE UNNAMED DISCIPLE

JUDY SALISBURY

JUDY SALISBURY

MORE THAN DEVOTION

FIFTY-DAYS OF REMEMBRANCE AND RESOLVE

Calamity Care

My 31-Day Spiritual Guide to Thrive

JUDY SALISBURY

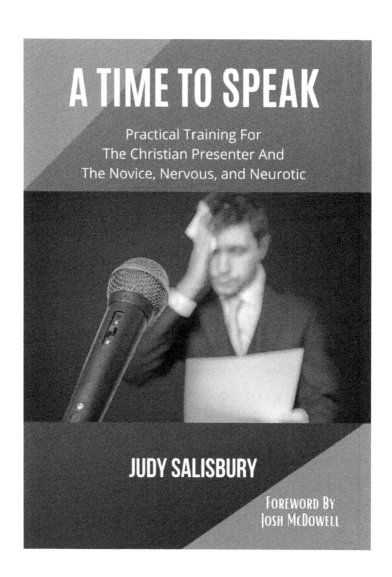

A TIME TO SPEAK

Practical Training For
The Christian Presenter And
The Novice, Nervous, and Neurotic

JUDY SALISBURY

FOREWORD BY
JOSH MCDOWELL

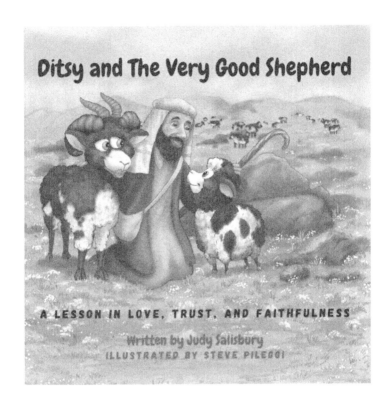

Ditsy and The Very Good Shepherd

A LESSON IN LOVE, TRUST, AND FAITHFULNESS

Written by Judy Salisbury

ILLUSTRATED BY STEVE PILEGGI

Made in the USA
Middletown, DE
04 March 2022

62091825R00086